Fetal Alcohol Syndrome/Effect

Fetal Alcohol Syndrome/Effect: Developing a Community Response

edited by
Jeanette Turpin and Glen Schmidt

Fernwood Publishing • Halifax

Editing: Douglas Beall
Design and production: Beverley Rach
Printed and bound in Canada by: Hignell Printing Limited

A publication of:
Fernwood Publishing
Box 9409, Station A
Halifax, Nova Scotia
B3K 5S3

The authors' proceeds from this publication will be donated to nonprofit organizations supporting children with FAS/E.

We are grateful to the Ministry for Children and Families of the Province of British Columbia for financial support provided for this publication.

Fernwood Publishing Company Limited gratefully acknowledges the financial support of the Ministry of Canadian Heritage and the Canada Council for the Arts for our publishing program.

Canadian Cataloguing in Publication Data

Turpin, Jeanette

    Fetal alcohol syndrome/effect

    Includes bibliographical references.
    ISBN 1-55266-011-7

1. Fetal alcohol syndrome -- Canada.　I. Schmidt, Glen.　II. Title.

RG629.F45T87 1999　　618.3'268　　C99-950013-9

Contents

Acknowledgements

We are grateful to Jeremy Berland of the Ministry for Children and Families in British Columbia. Without his interest and support, this book would not have been possible.

We would like to acknowledge the contribution of a young child with FAS who created the artwork on the cover. It is a picture of a child facing a large wave of water. The child said that the wave represents FAS overcoming communities. However, the child was quick to point out that she is smiling because she has learned ways to deal with her diability and she has a supportive and caring community.

Thanks also to the folks at Fernwood Publishing: Douglas Beall for editing, Beverley Rach for design and production, Jackie Logan for promotion and the publisher, Errol Sharpe.

About the Contributors

Joanne Alexander is a registered nurse who specializes in community health in Fort St. James, British Columbia. She came from northern Ontario and received her nursing education at Sault College, Dalhousie University and the University of Victoria. She has spent most of her twenty-two years in the nursing field, working in remote communities throughout northern Canada.

Michael Anthony Hart is a member of Fisher River Cree Nation in Manitoba and an assistant professor with the University of Manitoba Faculty of Social Work at Thompson. In addition to working with First Nations peoples in many parts of Canada, particularly Manitoba and the Yukon, he has worked in an employed and voluntary capacity to address issues associated with substance abuse.

Marie Hay has worked as a pediatrician on three continents—Europe, Africa and North America. She is a clinical associate professor with the University of British Columbia. In her work as a community pediatrician in northern British Columbia, she has evaluated many hundreds of children who suffer the sequelae of prenatal alcohol exposure.

Kathy Jones is the school consultant and community trainer with the Interagency FAS/E Program in Winnipeg, Manitoba. Through her role there, she provides advocacy and support to birth, adoptive and foster families raising alcohol-affected children. She provides workshops and consultations for schools, child protection agencies and community agencies on strategies for working with alcohol-affected children and their families. At home, Kathy is the foster parent of a daughter with FAE.

Anne Lindsay is an assistant professor of education at the University of Northern British Columbia. She has taught in inner-city Toronto, West Africa, and a First Nations school in northern Ontario. She has also supervised student teachers in schools in Victoria and taught in the British Columbia adult basic education program on northern Vancouver Island. Her research interests span the topics of First Nations education, classroom discourse, curriculum theory and educational policy.

Donna Preston is an elementary school teacher in northern British Columbia. Donna has taught for twenty-seven years across all levels of elementary school and has also taught as a faculty associate in a teacher education program. Her research interests include children with language and learning disabilities, and patterns of classroom discourse. She is presently engaged in graduate studies at the University of Northern British Columbia.

Glen Schmidt is an assistant professor of social work at the University of Northern British Columbia. He has worked as a social worker for twenty years, most of that time in child welfare and mental health programs in northern Manitoba. He is especially interested in service delivery issues that affect social workers and people living in northern and isolated communities.

Pat Short is a community health nurse in Fort St. James, British Columbia. She originates from Saskatchewan and is a graduate of St. Paul's Hospital in Saskatoon and Dalhousie University. She has twenty-seven years of nursing experience, the majority of it spent in the small northern communities where she loves to work. She has worked in northern British Columbia, Saskatchewan, Newfoundland, the Yukon and the Northwest Territories.

Gordon Ternowetsky is a professor of Social Work and the coordinator of the Child Welfare Research Centre at the University of Northern British Columbia. He publishes in the areas of social policy, income inequality, poverty and the welfare state. His recent books include *Remaking Canadian Social Policy: Social Security in the Late 1990s* (Fernwood, 1996) and *Child and Family Policies: Struggles, Strategies and Options* (Fernwood, 1997), both edited with Jane Pulkingham; and *Unemployment and Welfare: Social Policy and the Work of Social Work* (Garamond, 1990), edited with Graham Riches.

Jeanette Turpin is a social worker in adult forensic psychiatry in Prince George, B.C. Her previous experience has been in northern and remote child welfare practice. She has also worked for the Child Welfare Research Centre at the University of Northern British Columbia, where she engaged in a number of research projects related to fetal alcohol syndrome and fetal alcohol effects.

Kee Warner is a lone parent caregiver to adopted and foster children. Daughter of educators, Kee enjoys working with families and professionals, sharing her personal knowledge of behavioural and social issues associated with prenatal exposure to alcohol. She is currently at work on a book to help peers and extended family understand and enjoy people with alcohol-related disabilities. Kee lives with her family on a rural acreage west of Prince George, B.C.

Robert J. Williams is a clinical psychologist at the Addiction Centre, Foothills Hospital, Calgary, Alberta. His current research concerns the causes and treatment of adolescent drug abuse. Prior to this, he spent ten years as a psychologist with Manitoba Health and Family Services in northern Manitoba. A significant part of this position involved providing clinical services to developmentally delayed children.

Introduction

Jeanette Turpin and Glen Schmidt

The harmful effects of alcohol consumption during pregnancy have been recognized for many centuries. Prohibition against consumption by expectant mothers appears in ancient literature such as the Bible (Judges 13: 7) and, clearly, people have long had an awareness of a connection between birth abnormalities and alcohol consumption. However, precise understanding of the concept of fetal alcohol syndrome (FAS) and the more subtle fetal alcohol effects (FAE) is relatively recent. It was not until 1968 that research data empirically documented a definite relationship between alcohol consumption and developmental birth defects. In that year, Dr. Paul Lemoine and his colleagues in Nantes, France, published the results of a study of 127 children born to alcoholic mothers. The contents of the study described four characteristic abnormalities: (1) very peculiar faces, (2) increased frequency of malformation, (3) psychomotor disturbances and (4) considerable retardation of growth and height (Elliot and Johnson 1983). However, these findings were largely ignored until 1973, when similar research results appeared in the United States.

Since that time the relationship between alcohol abuse and birth defects has been clearly established. It has also become apparent that not everyone exhibits the full-blown syndrome and some people exhibit a partial range of characteristics known as fetal alcohol effects. The research has not established a safe level of alcohol consumption for pregnant women and it is fair to say that abstinence during pregnancy is the only certain way to avoid risking damage to the fetus.

Actual prevalence rates are difficult to determine, as diagnoses of fetal alcohol syndrome or fetal alcohol effects are not made through examination of genetic markers or any kind of definitive test procedure. Diagnosis relies on obtaining a history of the mother's alcohol consumption during pregnancy and subjective interpretation of the physical and behavioural characteristics consistent with fetal alcohol syndrome/fetal alcohol effects (FAS/E). Often this information is unavailable, and even when the information is provided, the syndrome may not be recognized (Little et al. 1990). As a result, the incidence of FAS has to be estimated and this estimate is currently cited at 1–3 per 1,000 births in North America (Smitherman 1994). It is abundantly clear in some communities, especially those in isolated and remote regions, that the prevalence rate is much higher and has to be considered a major health and education issue (Robinson, Conry and Conry 1987; Asante 1981).

Introduction

The prevalence rate cited by Smitherman is an estimate and it must be emphasized that it is difficult to establish accurate prevalence statistics. The research needed to gather this type of data must be conducted with sensitivity and collaboration. In the case of FAE, the behaviours associated with this label are contiguous with a variety of other issues, both individual and social, and this can further confound a conclusive diagnosis and resulting prevalence statistics.

It is clear that much work remains to be done in the area of recognition and diagnosis if those affected by FAS/E are to receive help. However, even for those who have a diagnosis, effective intervention remains a problem. The reality is that many children who have FAS/E come from homes marked by poverty, substance abuse and general social disorganization. American studies by Streissguth and Guinta (1988) have found that up to 69 percent of the biological mothers of FAS children were dead by the time the children reached adolescence. In many instances, the children experience marked family upheaval and many are apprehended by child welfare authorities and raised in foster care. The difficult behaviours of these children often result in exhaustion of foster parents and subsequent placement breakdown. It is not uncommon for some children to experience multiple caregivers and moves from one foster home to another. This is frustrating for human service workers, who are beginning to see second and third generations of FAS/E children in the same extended family. Unless these patterns are changed, the problem will continue with all its devastating consequences.

Unfortunately, intervention strategies for FAS/E children and their caregivers are not simple and require a coordinated and sophisticated application of resources. This process begins by avoiding fixation of blame and recognizing that FAS/E is a community problem that has its roots in poverty, marginalization, ignorance and resulting despair. When these factors are recognized as structural issues, resources can be allocated in ways that will not stigmatize and further marginalize people.

The purpose of this book is to provide accessible and practical information to the front-line workers and caregivers of individuals who have FAS/E. There is also a particular focus on service issues as they relate to northern and remote communities which have a history of being underserviced. The material in this book draws heavily from front-line practitioners whose contributions, work and knowledge are frequently unrecognized.

Kee Warner is both a foster parent and an adoptive parent of FAS/E children. She is one of many unsung, committed caregivers whose love and dedication provides children with an opportunity to succeed in life. It is fitting that she contributes the first chapter to this book, as her account provides a realistic picture of what it is like to care for FAS/E children on a daily basis.

Diagnosis is of fundamental importance in understanding the reason for the behaviours associated with FAS/E. It is also a critical component in making the case for resources and services. The second chapter is contributed by Dr. Marie Hay, a consulting pediatrician, who has had extensive experience diagnosing children suspected of having FAS/E. Her experience is particularly important given the fact that much of her work is associated with northern and remote communities.

Dr. Robert J. Williams is a psychologist with extensive northern practice experience. In the third chapter, he provides an understanding of the role of psychological testing in diagnosing FAS/E. His personal practice experience has included extensive work with First Nations people, and he comments on some important considerations that must be brought to bear in cross-cultural practice.

The role of community is vital in addressing the issue of FAS/E, as it takes a whole community to raise a child. Joanne Alexander and Pat Short are public health nurses working with parents who have children in the early developmental stages. They contribute the fourth chapter and discuss the importance of developing a community-based approach that supports and nurtures children and parents.

As children move through the life cycle, they enter the formal public education system. It is often at this point that FAS/E is recognized for the first time. Children affected by maternal alcohol consumption face particular struggles in school which may exacerbate behavioural difficulties. These children present unique challenges to teachers and school administrators. Anne Lindsay and Donna Preston are educators who describe the educational challenges in regard to FAS/E children and recommend some possible strategies in the delivery of education programs.

FAS/E is an issue that affects all people in all social groups. It is a particular challenge in some First Nations communities where incidence may be high. Michael Anthony Hart is a First Nations social worker and educator who contributes the sixth chapter. He emphasizes the importance of understanding human diversity, especially the First Nations world view, when providing service for children and families affected by FAS/E.

It is clear that FAS/E is a complicated and difficult problem that requires intervention on a variety of levels. Kathy Jones is the foster parent of an FAE child and a community worker with an organization that provides service to families and children with FAS/E. In the seventh chapter she describes the need for multidisciplinary services within the community.

FAS/E is most prevalent among people and communities marginalized through poverty and other socio-economic conditions. In Chapter 8, Gordon Ternowetsky explores recent changes to Canada's social safety net that have a pronounced effect on the delivery of health and social services.

Introduction

The decline in services to Canada's poorest people is closely linked to the problem of FAS/E and limits the development of preventive policies.

Finally, Jeanette Turpin and Glen Schmidt have written about the issues and challenges associated with developing effective services for people in northern and remote communities. The available research tends to suggest that the incidence of FAS/E is higher in northern parts of Canada, and clearly northern regions do not boast the range of resources available to southern urban populations. Strategies related to case management must be revisited, and social workers who provide service in remote communities must expand the scope of their practices to ensure that clients' needs are addressed even when "expert" resources are not readily available. There are no easy solutions, but understanding the nature of the problem and the essential resource requirements are first steps toward effective management.

Parenting Children
with Fetal Alcohol Syndrome

Kee Warner

I am both a foster parent and an adoptive parent, and I reside in a small town in northern British Columbia. Currently I care for five children, ages 4–13, all of whom have problems which relate to prenatal exposure to alcohol. All five have been with me for more than three years. This is my personal account of what it's like to parent children who are referred to as having fetal alcohol syndrome/fetal alcohol effects, or FAS/E. As a family, we have had many opportunities to educate the public, and I hope we have made a difference in people's perceptions and expectations about kids who have problems that result from prenatal exposure to alcohol.

I try to start my day at 5:30 a.m. Some days this gives me a chance to shower, start breakfast and set the table before anyone else is out of bed. However, most days start with singing from the next bedroom as our earliest riser tries to quietly wake up someone to play with. He sleeps poorly and is usually awake for an hour or so around 1 a.m., so the night seems endless to him. His singing starts softly with familiar songs. His school anthem starts, "Build a road of peace before us. . . ." I wish for peace and quiet, but he gradually gets louder and more inventive. Hopefully he sings, "La de la, who is up? La de la, May is up. La de la, must I wonder what's for breakfast?" His morning routine chart is the only thing in the house he forgets. It has no finger-worn edges and it says wake-up time is 6 a.m. "La de la, Mom's up." The time is anywhere from 4:30 to 5:30.

Since he knows what everyone else is supposed to do, by 6:30 we're usually rolling. "Ellen, it's 6:30, time to eat, you're supposed to be dressed already. Mom, its 6:30 and Ellen's not dressed yet." Even May, the youngest, at four, follows her chart fairly well. All the kids move through their morning routines with relative ease, weaving the fabric for the day with their comings and goings, showering, dressing and eating. This routine has been practised for three years and, unless I get up too late or someone else gets up too early, this is the smoothest part of the day. I hover, preventing distractions, reminding one child that she was on the way to the bathroom to brush her teeth and another that dumping both bags of building blocks on the playroom floor is not on her morning list. Everyone's clothing has been chosen and laid out in order the night before. Right now we're experimenting with the two oldest girls trading outfits some mornings, and so far they have been able to handle this variance in their routine.

We live by routines. Lists and charts are commonplace around our house. Each child has a morning routine chart in their bedroom. Once I removed a bathroom chart drawn with washable markers that had become illegible due to streaks and unfathomable smudges. Everyone washed their hands and flushed the toilet anyway, so I thought it wasn't needed. The smell told me I was wrong when we got home that afternoon. When I asked the children how they could tell what to do from a chart that was torn and blurred, one answered that she could figure out the pictures by running her fingers over them. Another said he could tell there were six pictures and counted until he could remember all six things to do. We made two new charts, one for each bathroom, and the smell stayed away.

All of our charts have the time in three ways: a picture of a round clock face, words and numbers. Sometimes we also put the words in two ways. For instance, "seven forty" and "twenty minutes before eight." I don't really know if all these ways of naming time help, as only my seven-year-old (the one who thinks it is morning and he has let me sleep in a long time when he wakes me at 4:15) can consistently tell time. Ellen, who is eleven, started blabbering in frustration one night when I said she needed to have her chores finished when I got home at five. She thought I meant five in the morning. However, when they have one finger on the chart and the other hand pointing at the clock counting minutes, they can figure out where they are in the day.

Our charts have cartoons in the middle column and then a column for words. This works well, not only for our littlest one, who doesn't read much yet, but for all the kids, who may function at various age levels throughout the day. If they can't read right now, the picture of a jacket will remind them to wear one. They all get a tremendous laugh when I draw the pictures. I hear echoes of the ridicule they hear when they say, "You call that a chair?" It's an opportunity for me to model a response that takes the sting out of a putdown. "Yeah, I'd better put some blocks under this leg or whoever sits there will fall into their soup." Usually we draw the charts together, or one of the children will redo a chart at craft time. The older kids make lists: lists of their homework, names of people they will see tomorrow, names of the people they saw today, lists of the clothes they will need for an outing, lists of the foods they like or don't like, grocery lists. They often carry lists in their pockets and refer to them when needed.

The charts are our only wall decorations. When we first moved to this house with its dark wood walls, I put up my paintings and photographs. The kids became rowdier. I took them down and the kids calmed down.

Our chart gets us all to the front hall. If the morning has not gone smoothly, or even if we are ready too early and there is unstructured time, trouble shows up in a traffic jam at the front door.

"Ellen took two apples."

"Mine has a bruise."

"Well, you have it then."

"Who gave you a bruise?"

"Get away, I can't tie my shoes while you're talking to me."

"Quit yelling, I can't see my list."

Morning

6 A.M. Six o'clock		Time to wake up
6:30 Six thirty		May and Tom eat breakfast Big kids ① shower ② get dressed ③ eat
7:00 Seven o'clock		Brush your teeth Comb your hair
7:40 Seven forty Twenty minutes before eight		Hugs and on the bus

Afternoon and Evening		
3:00 P.M. Three o'clock		School is out You and your pack on the bus
3:20 P.M. Twenty minutes past three		Empty and put away your pack and containers
3:30 P.M. Half past three		Play
4:45 P.M. Quarter to five		Wash for supper Tara and Penny set the table
5:00 P.M. Five o'clock	Yum!	Supper
5:30 P.M. Half past five	1st 2nd	Ellen and Tom clear the table Homework Play
6:50 P.M. Half past six	SH!	Quiet time and bath time begin

Then comes "Mom!" from all five voices at once.

Finally, we are all out the door. We line up for goodbye hugs and leave the relative haven of "just us."

All five kids go to the same school. It is small, fewer than eighty-five students in eight grades. And it is rural, although some kids come from town on the bus. Our family couldn't have a better school situation. The teachers and assistants, parent advisory council, the principal and parent volunteers all work to understand and to adapt programs for my kids, and even the other students have had a half-day presentation on FAS/E. Although my kids aren't the only ones, the percentage of alcohol-affected kids in their school is not as great as in some of the town schools where there is an estimated 20–30 percent.

Our local FAS/E group puts on a lot of workshops that generally receive a very good response from the educators. Everyone involved with the kids, even the bus driver and janitor, need to know how they work and why. Our regular bus driver forgot one day and left his window-washer spray bottle within reach behind his seat. Soon the back of his head was being polished. One frequent substitute driver greeted my friendliest, most boisterous child (to some people's annoyance) on the first day back from Christmas vacation with "Sit down and shut up!" Fortunately there was a teacher there to mediate. Over the next three months we still had incidents of one child after another pointing a finger in someone's face and repeating that bus driver's commands. For some reason, bad examples take only one hearing and they are learned. Good examples take forever.

As good as our school is, I'm always somewhat anxious until we are all home together again. One day, returning to my office and checking for messages, I found three calls from the school in the previous forty-five minutes. Two messages read, "Principal called, please call back." The third said, "There has been an incident at the school and your daughter is suspended. Please come and get her now." The drive to school takes twenty minutes. While I drove, I searched for clues from the previous night. No, nothing happened. We were happy and calm. The morning went by without incident. I don't think I forgot her medication or her hug.

When I arrive, her body is calm, slumped, dejected, and her eyes show panic. "But it was just a 'deliberant,' Mom. It was deliberant." Feeling as much a criminal as my daughter, I am ushered into the principal's office. "Penny is suspended because she intended to cause physical harm to another student," he states. "Although no adult saw her hit the boy with the shovel, they did see the wrestling match that followed. The boy was simply trying to protect himself."

Penny's written account of the incident said, "I accidentally hit Jake in the head with the shovel and he pushed my back down and we wrestled in the hallway." The principal was apologetic, especially about having to send Penny home. We both had been working hard with the teacher to keep Penny from being sent even to the hall. However, since it was considered an intentional attempt to hurt Jake, I knew a suspension was inevitable.

I'll never be able to be the parent who indignantly says, "My child would never do that!" They would. They do. Penny, however, usually confesses when she's done something and even sometimes when she hasn't. She adores her principal. Perhaps the look in her eyes was shame, but fear was what it seemed like to me. I asked her to tell us what had happened. She read her written account out loud. Afterwards, I said, "Penny, where was Jake when you hit him with the shovel?"

"In the head, but it was accidiberal."

"Where was he . . ."

"Near the front doors," she interrupted.

". . . standing in relation to you?"

"OUTSIDE!"

I asked her to stand up and show us how they were both standing. Calming immediately, Penny stood.

"Show me how you were holding the shovel."

Penny pantomimed lifting the shovel to her shoulder, the blade behind her. I asked if Jake was standing in front of her or behind. She turned and pointed behind. The principal was patiently watching. He seemed a little less tense as well. So was I, as the picture began to become more clear and less sinister.

"How did you know it was Jake behind you?"

Penny pours out the whole scene. "I didn't know where he was. I didn't hear anybody. The shovel bumped somebody and then Jake was holding my back down and I couldn't stand up and we started wrestling. I said I was sorry, Mom. I told Jake I was sorry. I don't want to be sent home."

"How did you know you hit Jake in the head with the shovel?"

"The principal told me, but I didn't know that. I didn't mean to hit him anywhere. I didn't know he was there. We're friends now. Can't I stay at school?"

"When you fight at school you have to go home. What can you learn from today?"

"Not to fight at school."

"Yes, and what else? What can you do? What can you do when you have the shovel?"

"Not have the shovel."

"How do I carry my axe at home?"

"With the sharp part down."

"What about if you are carrying the shovel and people are close to you?" I ask.

"Carry the sharp part straight down like this" she responds. "Then I wouldn't have hit Jake in the head. But I didn't know he was there. I didn't hear him."

"How far away do I stand when I'm using my axe?"

"As far as you can reach with it."

"How do you know besides hearing if someone is too close?"

"I don't know. I didn't hear him."

"What else can you use besides your ears?"

"My eyes. I can look to see if someone is too close."

"Right. You learned to look and listen for people around you and you learned to carry the shovel with the sharp part aimed down."

"Jake and I are talking and we're friends now. Can I stay?"

"What about the wrestling?"

"Oh yeah. If I fight at school I have to go home. But we're not fighting now. I won't fight anymore. I guess I have to go home anyway, but can I come back tomorrow?"

We all relaxed. What appeared from Penny's admission to be a senseless deliberate act of hostility was now recognized as an innocent accident which may be avoided next time, at least with the shovel.

Predictable, structured, supervised parts of the school day generally go well. The three middle kids take Ritalin on school days. They all showed the dramatic change from frustration to success, from no friends to birthday party invitations, from inability to remain still long enough to hear instructions to being able to focus and finish assignments which Ritalin can sometimes facilitate. They are all bright and capable kids. Penny doesn't read well, but the others read at or above their age levels. Tara can't organize her way out of a wet paper bag, but she can multiply as fast and accurately as anyone else in her class. "What does that mean, Mom? I can't fit in a paper bag, can I?" They are all good-looking kids, prettier than most (I may be biased). They are friendly and bubbly, enthusiastic and they never quit trying. They never hold a grudge and sulk only when they can't remember. But this is still a popular characteristic with some of their teachers.

They like everybody, which brings me to my next worry. They will tell their life stories to anybody who will listen and they will run up and hug a near stranger. The meter-reader lady used to love to come to our house. Out would come tumbling four charming children to greet her with hugs and greetings appropriate to a long-lost friend. She wondered why I would deprive her and the kids of this affection. I explained to her that they need constant reminders to differentiate between family and acquaintances, and to know what behaviour is appropriate toward friends and strangers. The kids and I then worked on some more lists: lists of the people we hug, lists of the people we talk to if they call, and a list of the people we tell, "Just a minute, I'll call my mom." They gamely started on this last list, but my seven-year-old, who finds writing very difficult, realized quickly the list was too long for him to write. The others weren't convinced at first. It took half a page or more before they realized everyone else in the world was on the third list. We all talk about friends and strangers at least once a week. When the meter reader now comes for tea and a visit, she holds her arm out to show the kids where to stand while they are talking to her. She tells them hugs are for your grandparents and parents and the family that lives in your house. They have had the streetproofing program at school. Still, there was one very surprised bus porter when Ellen jumped at him and gave him a huge hug. She remembered him from a fifteen-minute bus ride to the airport eight days before. The older girls would get in a car with anybody, given an unsupervised chance.

So we practice and rehearse as often as we can. We are fortunate to have friends who are willing to learn with us, to come for dinner, to take us fishing, to teach us how to fix bicycles. These are things that other families may take for granted, but it takes very special people to have the patience and understanding that we need.

A recent and frequent visitor remarked on the disruption that just one familiar but extra person can cause for the children. That evening they forgot to sit at the table, to talk one at a time, to eat with their mouths closed and to talk with their mouths empty. We had a spilled plate, a chair tipped over and one child so embarrassed she ran out of the room in a temper. Our friend will come another time. The children will have forgotten and we'll try again.

We schedule one dinner out each month. We go early when the restaurant will be nearly empty and sit at the same table, which is away from most of the bustle. We go before our usual suppertime so no one is out of control due to hunger. I use many reminders to sit still, sit up, use your fork, use your best restaurant behaviour.

"Can I have money for the gumball machine?"

"No."

"Can I?"

"No."

The staff and the other patrons probably still think I'm too strict. They used to try to tell me that it was okay with them if the kids wandered around and looked out the windows, talked to the cook, borrowed the waiter's order pad and played catch with the crayons. I disagreed often enough that they gave up. Other people who know my children are surprised that we can eat out at all. With clear, consistent and familiar rules, the kids have a good time and behave well.

Unscheduled restaurant stops are very different. They can be the disasters that other people expect from us. One late lunch at an unfamiliar restaurant went like this. Everyone was hungry, which always means poor behaviour. The chairs were plastic and slippery, so no one could sit still anyway. My oldest daughter slid down in her chair, hid behind her menu and pretended she was anywhere else but there. She wouldn't let the waitress take the menu even after we ordered. Everyone else complained loudly until the food came. My son climbed up on the table to get fries from another child's plate. He thought they were not as hot as his. The people at the next table smiled and tried hard to continue eating. They remarked that they were grandparents and understood. One child sat in my lap to eat while I fed another one. The kids calmed down as they ate and everything was fine until little May slipped in her chair and brought her fist down on her fork trying to catch her balance. It flew precisely at the back of the nice grandfather at the next table. He pretended not to notice. The waitress surreptitiously called the cook over to watch. My daughter behind the menu walked blindly out the door, clutching the menu firmly. The owner came over to the table to collect our money and ask for the menu back. My son went on eating, oblivious to everything. May tiptoed carefully over to the next table, apologized and tripped over one of their chairs. I tipped well and waited about two years before returning to eat there. Really I prefer eating at home. Some days even that isn't safe and predictable.

One Friday night I had the washing machine unhooked and pulled into the doorway of the kitchen. The two oldest girls were cooking macaroni and cheese. Laundry baskets surrounded my work space and spilled into the kitchen as the machine had not been working all week. Something was happening the next morning and we needed certain clothes washed. I was trying to direct the cooks to read the instructions out loud so that each could say and hear them. They were having trouble getting all the way to the end of the instructions.

"How much is three cups?"

"Do you put the noodles in first?"

"Turn off the burner. That box is going to burn!"

The three younger children were parked at the table with books, crayons and the craft box. Someone, somehow, had the bowl of carrot sticks in the middle of the glue and construction paper. Maybe we needed clean clothes because the Queen was coming to visit the next day. It had to be at least that important, whatever it was. Of course, no one was really colouring, reading or even sitting at the table. Too much strange stuff was going on around them. Laundry and meal preparation are usually as unnoticeable as wallpaper.

"What's this thing for, Mom? Is this what makes the noise in the washer? Can I have this for my craft project?"

"No, those are the vice grips."

"How many cups of water?"

The chaos is amazingly amicable. I asked them to be calm and patient. The kids are disturbed but trying hard to cooperate. As I was insisting that the cooks do the math themselves to figure out three cups times three boxes, the doorbell rang. An acquaintance asked where the Smiths live. I didn't know but thought our neighbours would, so he left to ask them. The kids all wanted to know who that was. I said it was Mr. Arloe. It took several times of me saying it for them to get it right and then they started playing word games with it. I stopped the word games, suggested that a bigger pot was necessary for nine cups of water, silently congratulated myself because the kids took his visit in stride and went back to repairing the machine. The doorbell rang again. Mr. Arloe was back to use the phone. I told him to come on in, to leave his shoes on as the floor was full of wrenches and such. My son either didn't hear or didn't comprehend the part about the shoes and the next thing I know he has put his own shoes on with unprecedented speed and is stomping on Mr. Arloe's feet as he tries to use our telephone. Two boxes of macaroni hit the floor and tried to escape into the laundry baskets, the tool box and under the cupboards. In my haste to save Mr. Arloe's, feet and with the word games still echoing in my head, I yelled "Arloe!" instead of telling my son Tom to get away from Mr. Arloe's feet. One of the cooks started having a tug of war with a pad of construction paper at the table, and the other fled in embarrassment. May was quietly taking the front door apart with the vice grips. Mr. Arloe maintained a saintly calm while his feet were pummeled until he finished his telephone conversation. He pretended people shout at him every day while their kids stomp his feet. He thanked me graciously for the use of the phone, dodged the still escaping macaroni, put the knob back on the door and left. I didn't even have time to wonder what stories he might tell at his party, as I fished one child and one packet of cheese powder out of the washing machine and went about getting each child settled in turn. I think we did eat that night, but it wasn't long before we had a new washing machine.

Most meals aren't like these, but behaviour and hunger are closely linked. I eliminate as much confusion as I can at mealtime. We rotate breakfasts, eating pancakes with fruit and yogurt one morning, toasted egg sandwiches and fruit the next, hot cereal with fruit and toast and then back to pancakes. If for some reason we are rushed and have cold cereal for breakfast, I can expect a call from the school by recess. A cold breakfast just doesn't give my crew what they need. Lunch at school is always a battle. Without close supervision the kids just don't take the time to eat. We all know if someone didn't eat their lunch because that's the someone who gets in trouble on the bus ride home, is cranky at home and for whom even washing hands and face before dinner is a struggle. If we insisted that it is that somebody's turn to set the table, we'd never eat. We just put her or him at the table with carrot sticks or whatever else is handy and work around them.

Suppers match the day of the week. We have meatloaf on Monday, every Monday, spaghetti on Tuesday and so forth. If I get tired of some dish (the kids never seem to), we have a family meeting and decide on a change. Then we change our chart a week or so ahead of time. It still takes a few days for everyone to catch up to the change and someone will be insisting that it must be Saturday because we're having tuna casserole on Wednesday. When it hasn't recently changed, this schedule helps all through the week. At supper the kids will know who has art class and who has computer the next day because of what we are eating.

We also have a lot of snacks. My kids have trouble sitting long enough to eat a whole meal. They don't recognize when they are hungry or when they have had enough to eat. I keep an endless supply of apples and other fruit, popcorn, yogurt, rice cakes and soup. My two middle kids look like they never eat.

Everything we work on: our charts, teachers using the very same phrases that I use at home, me using the exact phrases the teachers use at school. All our structure and predictability are aimed at keeping the kids in contact with the world around them, at continuity, to allow them steady progress through the day. One day the two older girls were discussing a party and suddenly neither of them could remember the name of one of their friends. One said the hole in her memory was "like a wall" while the other said "it is like being full of nothing." They agreed it was a wall of nothing. It is the same when they lose their memories of what is happening right now. When the continuity is lost, they are completely lost; afraid to move, afraid to stay still; not knowing what to say, unable to say anything. Their actions become random and impulsive, making no sense even to themselves. Some of these behaviours are having temper tantrums, fabricating answers, taking things belonging to someone else, being unable to hear and act on the simplest request, jumping up from the table and running into the next room and then coming to a stop not knowing how or why, perseverating, interrupting, talking incessantly or banging into people without noticing. Ellen falls to the floor and her feet wave in the air above her head. "I can't," she wails before I've even finished asking her to sit in her chair. May whines, "I want just rice," all the way through supper and through her bath and story and then in her sleep, whether she has had just rice or not. Penny comes home from an overnight at her best friend's house with a sandwich bag of bracelets. "I don't know how they got there. My friend doesn't want them anyway." These moments are embarrassing for everyone. Nobody learns anything good from them and usually someone else picks up the behaviour as well. So we try to find ways to keep connected and avoid getting lost.

When we are working on a problem, trying to remember a friend's name, to resolve a temper tantrum or to plan what to do if something goes wrong at tomorrow's basketball game, the girls say we are building bridges through the wall of nothing. If they can touch or hear or smell or see something familiar and safe, they can find their way.

The times when they get most lost, have the least structure and experience the most disruption is when my foster children have visits with their parents. Unfortunately, they too may have problems from prenatal exposure to alcohol. Coming home after a weekend of ice cream and chips, no real bedtime, TV all night and no boundaries (for children or adults) is a mixture of rebellion and relief. Once back with me, they all head straight to the afternoon chart.

"I'm hungry, we didn't have supper."

"We can't have a snack, it's after our bedtime."

"It can't be bedtime, it's ten o'clock, not nine o'clock."

"What day is it, anyway?"

How much harder it must be for them during these times to find a way through the emotional wall of nothing.

By 6:30 p.m. I don't know whether quiet time is more important for the kids or for me. I read bedtime stories in two shifts, first for the little kids (although the big kids find excuses to sit close). I tuck the younger ones into bed. Their bedrooms are very plain, almost empty, but each item has to be in exactly the right place before they can settle. "Teddy doesn't like to sleep in that corner of the bed. That's Shadow's place." One sleeps. The other one tiptoes, or so he thinks, to where he can hear the big kids' stories. I spend half an hour or so with each in turn, talking over the day and tucking them in. I carry Mr. Tiptoe to his bed. It is often 11 p.m. before Tara, my night owl, is ready to give in to sleep. It is the worst time of the day for her if she doesn't have my undivided attention. "Mom, I have to tell you something. What are we having for breakfast? What is your middle name? Do you like mine?" If we miss or shorten this ritual, she has a temper tantrum which often wakes the others. She is then remorseful for the rest of the sleepless night.

If tomorrow's a hot cereal day, I put the crockpot on to cook while I sleep. While I write my daily notes, I think over the day. Some days are pretty discouraging—those when I have failed to provide the continuity and someone has gotten lost in the nothingness. Then I have to model positive thinking for myself. Some days, when the kids have all been successful it feels great. Like tonight when little May suggested, "Mom has to do her homework now, so let's all be quiet." Tonight I can agree with Penny when she says they are going to have a good life.

· 2 ·

A Practical Roadmap
for the Imperfect
But Practical-minded Clinician

Marie Hay

This chapter aims to provide a practical, clinically based approach to the diagnosis and treatment of children and families suffering from the chronic condition of fetal alcohol syndrome/fetal alcohol effects (FAS/ E). It is aimed specifically at hard-pressed, overworked, time-strapped and imperfect clinicians who work in remote and rural areas of northern Canada. Many of these clinicians are on the front lines of the FAS/E war and are heroically trying to do the best they can, with little or no other professional resources available to them. Many such clinicians feel inadequate or insecure about diagnosing FAS/E, especially when they compare themselves to the "perfectionism" practiced at relatively well-resourced tertiary teaching centres. Such centres are usually situated at a great distance from the northern FAS/E war zone. Like parents who need reassurance that they do not have to be "perfect parents" but just "good enough," clinicians need to know that they do not always have to make the "perfect diagnosis." It is okay to give a "good enough" opinion based on our valuable clinical expertise. By making a "good enough" diagnosis, we can help patients and their families to have their needs identified and attended to in an expeditious manner.

Background
In 1968 a pediatrician in rural France, Dr. Lemoine, published the first description of children with what is now known as fetal alcohol syndrome. In a later conversation with noted FAS researcher Ann Streissguth, Dr. Lemoine said, "Because I am not a scientist but a clinician, I examine infants with my hands, my eyes, my ears. It is only in this manner that one can diagnose FAS. It is impossible to diagnose FAS from a list of lab results. It is necessary to handle and think about each infant individually and to have seen other children with FAS" (Streissguth 1994). As a clinician of similar sentiment, I find Dr. Lemoine's statement reassuring and encouraging.

A Practical Roadmap for the Clinician

It is important for the clinicians working in the northern and remote areas who are seeing large numbers of children with FAS/E to know what to look for on a child's body. When I speak of clinicians, I include all professionals who may be required to work with these children and their families—doctors, nurses, infant development workers, occupational therapists, speech and language pathologists, etc. We need to know the myriad of signs and symptoms of FAS/E. If we are only able to identify the tiny minority of "classic FAS" children, we miss the vast majority of those who are more subtly affected. Special-needs children and their families are put at a disadvantage when this subtle diagnosis is missed. Without a diagnosis, they will not benefit from early intervention services. These extra services assist in coping with the physical, neurodevelopmental, neurobehavioural and psychiatric symptoms of this chronic, lifelong disabling condition.

Clinician's Atlas for Exploring the World of FAS/E Landmarks

All of the following characteristics have been mentioned in the literature as occurring in children diagnosed as FAS/E. However, based solely on my clinical experience, I have categorized their occurrence on a continuum, from rare to very common.

General Areas

Very Common	*Less Common*
• Facial dysmorphism • Hirsutism	• Low birth weight, height and head circumference • Failure to thrive due to lack of adipose tissue • Postnatal linear growth retardation • High neonatal and infant death rates • High rate of SIDS

Fetal Alcohol Syndrome/Effect

Central Nervous System

Very Common	*Less Common*	*Rare*
• Cognitive impairment (but IQ can range up to 140)	• Neurological damage	• Brain heteropias, ectopias and lissencephaly
• Poor eye-hand coordination	• Mental deficiency	
• Dysfunctional memory, especially short-term	• Attention deficit disorder (ADD) *without* hyperactivity	• Neuro tube defects (spina bifida)
• Learning disabilities, especially with math and reading	• Irritability as an infant (nconsolable infant crying)	• Neuroblastoma
• Poor sequencing of commands	• Tremulousness	• Cerebellar hypoplasia
• Poor conceptualization of time during the day, week or month	• Microcephaly	• Acardia syndrome (absent corpus callosum)
	• Hypertonia	• Macrocephaly (hydrocephalus)
• Attention deficit hyperactivity disorder (ADHD)	• Poor infant sucking	• EEG abnormalities
• Poor frontal lobe function	• Seizures	• Cerebral palsy
• Hypotonia	• Pervasive development disorders	• Gait disorders
• Global or isolated developmental delays (fine motor, gross motor, speech, personal and social adaptation)		
• Sleep disorders		

Neurobehavioural Problems/Psychiatric Problems

Very Common

- Attention deficit hyperactivity disorder (ADHD)
- Sleep disorder
- Poor social adaptation with immaturity, intrusiveness, overtalkativeness
- Poor judgment
- Poor peer relationships
- "Victim" traits (easily taken advantage of, easily abused)
- School failure/ dropout
- Other nonspecific behavioural disorders
- Depression
- Later life addictions problems (sex, drugs, food, nicotine, alcohol)

Less Common

- Attention deficit disorder with no hyperactivity
- Conduct disorders
- Obsessive/compulsive disorders
- Eating disorders
- Juvenile delinquency
- Sexual disorders
- Oppositional defiant disorder
- Perpetrators of abuse on other children, either physical or sexual
- Bipolar disease

Rare

- Autism
- Psychopathy
- Schizophrenia

Fetal Alcohol Syndrome/Effect

Craniofacial

Very Common	*Less Common*	*Rare*
• Midface hypoplasia (flat face)	• Abnormal head shape	• Abnormal tongue furrowing
• Dental problems (malocclusion, malalignment, hypoplastic enamel, dental caries)	• Microcephaly	• Abnormal sutures as a newborn
	• Malar hypoplasia	
	• Cleft palate	
	• Cleft chin	
• Short nose (often anteverted)	• Cleft lip	
	• Migrognathia (small chin)	
• Hypoplastic philtrum (often long)	• Retrognathia (recessed chin)	
• Thin upper vermillion border	• Bifid uvula	
	• Antimongoloid slant to eyes	
• High-arched palate	• Bushy eyebrows with or without synophrys	
• Thin or thick upper lip		
• Small or wide mouth		
• Flat nasal bridge		

Ears

Very Common	*Less Common*
• Eustachian tube dysfunction (recurrent serious otitis media)	• Bilateral seninsineural hearing loss (direct ototoxicity)
• Auditory perceptual difficulties leading to learning difficulties	• Poor vestibular proprioceptive coordination
• Low-set ears	• Microtia (small ears)
• Posteriorly rotated ears	• Abnormally shaped ears
• Outset ears	• Adherent or asymmetrical ears

A Practical Roadmap for the Clinician

Eyes

Very Common	*Less Common*	*Rare*
• Decreased visual acuity • Telecanthus (widely spaced eyes) • Short palprebral fissures (small slit to the eyes) • Ptosis (droopy eyes) • Myopia • Hyperopia • Strabismus • Astigmatism • Ambylopia	• Increased tortuosity of the retinal vasculature • Micropthalmia (small eyes) • Nystagmus	• Hypoplasia optic nerve • Corneal atresia • Cataracts • Glaucoma • Iris defects (coloboma)

Cardiovascular System

Very Common	*Less Common*	*Rare*
• VSD • ASD	• Co-artation of the aorta • Pulmonary stenosis • Mitral valve prolapse • Arrhythmias	• Tetralogy and pentalogy of Fallot

Liver

		Rare
		• Liver tumors • Dysplastic, fibrotic, cirrhotic liver

Fetal Alcohol Syndrome/Effect

Reticuloendothelial

Very Common

- Poor immune system with much increased respiratory problems and infections
- Increased allergy problems

Rare

- Cystic hygromas
- DiGeorge Syndrome
- Embryonal tumors (adrenal, hepatic, neuroblastoma)

Skeletal

Very Common

- Joint anomalies
- Hypoplastic nails (small nails)
- Brachydactyly (short, stubby fingers)
- Camptodactyly (double-jointed at tip of fingers)
- Clindactyly (medial incurving of fifth finger)
- Pectus excavatum/ carinatum
- Craniofacial asymmetry

Less Common

- Microcephaly
- Retarded bone age
- Scoliosis
- Synostosis of the long bones, especially the radioulnar
- Dislocated hips
- Carpal and tarsal coalition
- Small distal phalanges
- Coccygeal fovea
- Syndactyly (fused toes or fingers)
- Arachnodactyly (long fingers)
- Short neck
- Cervical spine anomalies
- Rib anomalies
- Wide gap between first and second toes
- Third toe overlapping second toe
- Short metacarpals
- Radial hypoplasia
- Small rib cage

Rare

- Copper-beaten skull on x-ray
- Amelia (absent limbs)
- Polydactyly (extra fingers or toes)
- Webbed neck
- Klipper-Feil Syndrome (cervical spine anomaly)
- Bifid xiphoid

Genital Urinary System

Very Common	*Less Common*	*Rare*
• Hydroceles • Inquinal hernias	• Undescended testicles • Hypospadias • Labial hypoplasia	• Small rotated kidneys • Horseshoe kidneys • Renal dysplasia • Hydronephrosis

Skin

Very Common	*Less Common*	*Rare*
• Abnormal dermato-glyphics (abnormal palmar creases) • Hemangiomata • Accessory nipples • Retracted nipples • Inverted nipples • Hypoplastic nipples • Hirsutism	• Hypo and hyper pigmentation • Low-set hairline • Abnormal hair	• Abnormal elastic skin with curtis laxis

Gastrointestinal

Very Common	*Rare*
• Umbilical hernia	• Atresias and malrotations • Diaphragmatic hernias • Abnormal wall hernias

The primary marker of FAS/E is the sum of the total "tally of anomalies," the cranio-facial defects being more specifically related to very early prenatal alcohol exposure. As the total number of anomalies increase, the more characteristic becomes the pattern of FAS/E. Two or more abnormal cranio-facial features are clinically significant.

Fetal Alcohol Syndrome/Effect

Some Roads Look Alike: The Differential Diagnosis
1. Environmental teratogenic look-alikes, involving prenatal exposure to:
*   Dilantin
*   Carbamezapine
*   Sodium valproate
*   Toluene

2. Chromosomal look-alikes
*   William's Syndrome
*   DiGeorge Syndrome
*   Russel Silver Syndrome
*   Correlia de Lange Syndrome

The clinician must constantly look for polydrug use and understand the compounding adverse effects that each drug has on the fetus, particularly if there is associated poor nutrition and poor health of the pregnant mother.

The Perfectionist's Roadmap
The following diagnostic criteria classifying children who have been prenatally exposed to alcohol have recently been documented by the Institute of Medicine (1996).

Fetal Alcohol Syndrome
1. **FAS with confirmed maternal alcohol exposure**
A. Confirmed maternal alcohol exposure.
B. Evidence of a characteristic pattern of facial anomalies that include features such as short palpebral fissures and abnormalities in the premaxillary zone (e.g., flat upper lip, flattened philtrum and flat midface).
C. Evidence of growth retardation, as in at least one of the following:
    *   low birth weight for gestational age
    *   decelerating weight over time not due to nutrition
    *   disproportional low weight to height.
D. Evidence of CNS neurodevelopmental abnormalities, as in at least one of the following:
    *   decreased cranial size at birth
    *   structural brain abnormalities (e.g., microcephaly, partial or complete)
    *   agenesis of the corpus callosum, cerebellar hypoplasia
    *   neurological hard or soft signs (as age appropriate), such as impaired fine motor skills

- neurosensory hearing loss, poor tandem gait, poor eye-hand coordination.

2. **FAS without confirmed maternal alcohol exposure**
   - B, C and D as above.

3. **Partial FAS with confirmed maternal alcohol exposure**
A. Confirmed maternal alcohol exposure.
B. Evidence of some components of the pattern of characteristic facial anomalies.
C. Evidence of growth retardation, as in least one of the following:
   - low birth weight for gestational age
   - decelerating weight over time not due to nutrition
   - disproportional low weight to height.
D. Evidence of CNS neurodevelopmental abnormalities, as in:
   - decreased cranial size at birth
   - structural brain abnormalities (e.g., microcephaly, partial or complete)
   - agensis of the corpus callosum, cerebellar hypoplasia
   - neurological hard or soft signs (as age appropriate), such as impaired fine motor skills, neurosensory hearing loss, poor tandem gait, poor eye-hand coordination.
E. Evidence of a complex pattern of behaviour or cognitive abnormalities that are inconsistent with developmental level and cannot be explained by familial background or environment alone, such as learning difficulties; deficits in school performance; poor impulse control; problems in social perception; deficit in higher-level receptive and expressive language; poor capacity for abstraction or metacognition; specific deficits in mathematical skills; or problems in memory, attention or judgment.
- Either C or D or E.

Alcohol-related Effects

These are clinical conditions in which there is a history of maternal alcohol exposure, and where clinical or animal research has linked maternal alcohol ingestion to an observed outcome.

There are two categories, which may co-occur. If both diagnoses are present, then both diagnoses should be rendered.

Fetal Alcohol Syndrome/Effect

1. Alcohol-related birth defects (ARBD)

List of congenital anomalies, including malformations and dysplasias:

Cardiac	Atrial septal defects Ventricular septal defects	Aberrant great vessels Tetralogy of Fallot
Skeletal	Hypoplastic nails Shortened fifth fingers Radioulnar synostosis Flexion contractures Camptodactyly	Clinodactyly Pectus excavatum and carinatum Klippel-Feil Syndrome Hemivertebrae Scoliosis
Renal	Aplastic, dysplastic, hypoplastic kidneys Horseshoe kidneys	Ureteral duplications Hydronephrosis
Ocular	Strabismus Retinal vascular anomalies	Refractive problems secondary to small globes
Auditory	Conductive hearing loss	Neurosensory hearing loss
Other	Virtually every malformation has been described in some patient with FAS. The etiologic specificity of most of these anomalies to alcohol teratogenesis remains uncertain.	

2. Alcohol-related neurodevelopmental disorder (ARND)

• Evidence of CNS neurodevelopmental abnormalities, as in any one of the following:

—decreased cranial size at birth

—structural brain abnormalities (e.g., microcephaly, partial or complete agenesis of the corpus callosum, cerebellar hypoplasia)

—neurological hard or soft signs (as age appropriate), such as impaired fine motor skills, neurosensory hearing loss, poor tandem gait, poor eye-hand coordination and/or

• Evidence of a complex pattern of behaviours or cognitive abnormalities that are inconsistent with development level and cannot be explained by familial background or environment alone, such as learning difficulties, deficits in school performance, poor impulse control, problems in social perception, deficits in higher level receptive and expressive language, poor capacity for abstraction or metacognition, specific deficits in mathematical skills, or problems in memory, attention or judgment.

Quick and Easy Roadmaps for the FAS/E Journey

1. Barclay's rating scale for ADHD.
2. Denver Developmental Evaluation Form or any you are familiar with.
3. DSM IV Criteria for Oppositional Defiant Disorder.
4. DSM IV Criteria for Conduct Disorder.
5. DSM IV Criteria for ADHD.
6. DSM IV Criteria for Pervasive Development Disorder.
7. Reynold's Pediatric Child Depression Scale.
8. *Smith's Recognizable Patterns of Human Malformation* (Jones 1997, fifth edition, chapter on "Normal Standards") gives the centiles for height, weight, head circumference, and face and hands measurements.
9. Centile Chart for Palpebral Fissures.
10. B.C. Children's Hospital Pediatric Drug Dosage Manual.
11. A ruler or tape measure.

Essential Provisions for the Journey
The clinician needs to be very respectful, understanding and have a truly open, non-blaming and non-shaming attitude. It is also important to carry lots of realistic hope for the future for the children and their families.

Medical Journey
The medical journey will take approximately two hours in the first instance. Further follow-up trips may be necessary to clarify complex situations. The following guide has been adapted from the one used by Dr. Christine Lock and her colleagues at the FAS Diagnostic Clinic of Sunnyhill Hospital in Vancouver, British Columbia.

1. Ordinary medical history:
- presenting complaints
- history of complaints
- past medical history
- family history
- nutritional history
- developmental history
- school history: How many schools has the child been in? What grade are they in? How are their academic and social skills in school? Try to get written documentation from the school about this.
- immunization history
- social history: Who are the biological parents? Who are all the siblings? What are their states of health? Who has custody and guardianship of the child? Since the child was born, how many placements has the child had? Of what duration and with whom? How many fathers/

father substitutes has the child had, and how many mothers/mother substitutes? How many changes of home has the child had? What is the original ethnic and cultural background of the child?
- current medication history
- allergy history
- sexual/menses history
- system review.

2. **Specific dysmorphic questions** (be direct in a kindly way but don't beat around the bush):
- Was this a surprise or planned pregnancy?
- How far along were you before you knew you were pregnant?
- Before you knew you were pregnant, when you were out partying, how much alcohol would you drink, a flat or __ flats? (flat = 24 beer)
- How many parties per week, three or four?
- How many coolers?
- How much hard liquor?
- How much nicotine did you smoke, one or two packs per day?
- How many tokes of marijuana per day, six or eight?
- Any LSD or magic mushrooms?
- Any cocaine or heroin?
- Any Ritalin or Valium?
- Any Tylenol 1s, 2s or 3s?
- Any other prescription medication like anti-convulsants? (Carbamazepine, Dilantin, Valproate, etc.)
- Any glue or gasoline sniffing?
- Before you knew you were pregnant, how many times per week would you get drunk?
- Any bad viruses during the pregnancy?
- Any bad bleeding during the pregnancy?
- How was your diet during the pregnancy? Did you eat quite a bit of junk food?
- How much care did you get from a nurse or doctor during the pregnancy?

Birth history:
- Where was the child born?
- What did the child weigh? Was the child term or preterm?
- Were there any perinatal problems?

Past obstetrical history:
- How many times have you been pregnant?
- How many children do you have alive?

- How many of these children currently live with you?
- Is there any history of birth defects on either side of the family?
- Any history of Sudden Infant Death Syndrome?
- Are there any other children fetal alcohol or drug–affected?

3. Ordinary medical examination:
- Height, weight, head circumference
- Blood pressure
- Head, eyes, ENT, CNS, Resp, CVS, ABD, Anal, Skin, GU
- Musculoskeletal
- Reticuloendothelial
- Note and list any and all dysmorphic features as previously outlined in the "Very Common" column of signs and symptoms of FAS/E.

4. The specific FAS/E examination (see *Smith's Recognizable Patterns of Human Malformation* [Jones 1997] for the centiles):
- Arm span (arms outstretched to tip of third finger (subtract O.C. from I.C. and divide by two)
- Lower body length (pubic bone to floor)
- Hand spread (fanned out on the table)
- Palm length
- Third finger length
- Total hand length (palm and third finger)
- Biparietal measurement (widest part of head above ears)
- Anterior-posterior measurement (nasal bridge to back of head)
- Outer canthal distance (A–F)
- Inner canthal distance (B–C)
- Horizontal face bar (palpebral fissure proportional to the inner canthal distance; in Caucasian and Blacks, usually 90–95%, less in Native American Indians and Asians; the palpebral fissure in FAS is usually less than inner canthus)
- Pubertal status (tanner I–V)
- Palpebral fissures (A–B) (C–F)
- Eyebrow to eyelid measurement
- Nose length (B–D)
- Philtrum (D–G)
- Midface length (B–E)
- Vertical face bar (nose length proportional to midface length; normal 60–70%; in FAS/E usually 55–65%)
- Ear length
- Degree of ear posterior rotation.

Neurological characteristics:

• Gait (walk, tiptoe, heel to toe)	0 1 2 3
• Stability (Romberg's)	0 1 2 3
• Movement (hopping on each foot, eyes open and closed)	0 1 2 3
• Balance (standing on each foot, eyes open and closed)	0 1 2 3
• Finger-nose (eyes open and closed)	0 1 2 3
• Heel-shin (eyes open and closed)	0 1 2 3
• Rapid alternating hand movements	0 1 2 3
• Deep tendon reflexes	0 1 2 3
• Eye grounds	0 1 2 3

Functional level ratings:

• Neurological impairment (composite of above)	0 1 2 3
• Cognitive ability (IQ and psychometric testing or grade functioning level)	0 1 2 3
• Behaviour disorder (hyperactivity)	0 1 2 3
• Affective disorder (depression, manic, oppositional)	0 1 2 3

These levels ratings are subjective interpretations (to a large extent based on experience) :

  0 = No signs or symptoms
  1 = Mild problem
  2 = Moderate problem
  3 = Severe problem (mentally deficient or extreme hyperactivity)

5.   Review as many school or other professional reports pertaining to the child as available.

6.   List all your confirmed and suspected diagnoses as thoroughly as possible. Don't be afraid to take the plunge. Trying to answer the following questions will help you a lot:
• Is this child on the FAS/E continuum/spectra?
• If yes, is he/she mild, moderate or severe?
• If the classic triad of FAS is present, then the child is automatically defined as severely affected. The rest usually fall into the mild or moderately affected category.
• Are any developmental delays present?
• Are any learning disabilities present?
• Is there any ADHD?
• Are any secondary disabilities present?
• Are there any other behavioural concerns (depression, etc.)?

- Is the child in care and therefore automatically an at-risk child?
- Has the child suffered from physical, emotional or sexual abuse?
- Has the child suffered significantly at the hands of the bureaucracy by being shifted repeatedly from pillar to post?
- Has the child/adolescent become involved with the criminal justice system?
- Is the child/adolescent leading a self-destructive lifestyle (alcohol, promiscuity, etc.)?
- Is there any evidence of acute or chronic post-traumatic stress?

7. Decide what investigations are needed:
- Optometric eye examination.
- Hearing test.
- If ADHD is suspected, TSH, lead levels, CBC and differential.
- If there is a suspicion of a particular problem, then a specific relevant test may be necessary (for example, if a seizure disorder is suspected, order an EEG, if a skeletal abnormality, then an x-ray).

8. Formulate a practical plan for the child and family to follow.
Bear in mind that by far the most important therapeutic intervention for FAS/E children is a stable, loving, structured, long-term family environment. This should be combined with a supportive and adaptable school educational system. If these two elements are not available, the journey is going to be rough for the clinician and hell for the child.

When deciding with the family on a plan of action, bear in mind that many affected families are already overwhelmed. We must not overtax them further by making them travel huge distances to see us, at immense cost and inconvenience, especially if we are providing them with inappropriate services lacking in cultural sensitivity. As clinicians, we should always be willing to adapt and be innovative, using and maximizing the local resources, which do not have to be "perfect" but only "good enough."

Practical Considerations at Particular Stages in the Life Cycle
For infants, 0–18 months:
- Does the child need the Infant Development Program for early stimulation and family support?
- Does the child need the rehabilitative services of a Child Development Centre/Family Enhancement Centre for physiotherapy, speech language pathology or occupational therapy?

For preschoolers, 0–5 years:
- Does the child need the rehabilitative services of an occupational therapist, physiotherapist or speech language pathologist?

- Does the child need to see a clinical psychologist for evaluation and behavioural management strategies?
- Does the child need a therapeutic preschool, head-start program or a community preschool staffed by early childhood educators familiar with children who have FAS/E?

For school children, 5–18 years:

- Does the child need mental health services, a clinical psychologist or a child psychiatrist?
- Does the child need ongoing extra help with physiotherapy, occupational therapy or speech language therapy through the school district?
- Does the child need IQ and psychometric testing through the school psychologist to pick up mental deficiency or learning disabilities?
- Does the child need to be involved with school counsellors?
- Are the school staff aware of the child's diagnoses and special needs?

For the family:

Peer support
Get the parents involved with their provincial FAS Resource Society (in British Columbia, it is located in Vancouver) and the support group known as CHADD (Children and Adults with Attention Deficit Disorder; national office address is Box 23007, Ottawa, Ontario, K2A 4E2).

Education
Ask the parents to go to the library and borrow books and videos on fetal alcohol syndrome/effects, ADHD, parenting, etc. Recommend the following books: *Solve Your Child's Sleep Problems*, by Richard Ferber, M.D. (1985); *Reaching Out to Your Children with FAS/E*, by Diane Davis (1994); *The ADHD Parenting Handbook*, by Colleen Alexander-Roberts (1994); *How to Talk So Kids Will Listen*, by Adele Faber and Elaine Mazlish (1980); *Putting on the Brakes*, by Patricia Quinn and Judith Stern (1991); *1-2-3 Magic*, by Thomas Phelan (1995); *The Broken Cord*, by Michael Dorris (1989); *Fantastic Antone Succeeds*, by Judith Kleinfeld and Siobhan Wescott (1993); *Your Hyperactive Child*, by Barbara Ingersol (1988); *Beyond Ritalin*, by Stephan Garber, Marianne Daniels Garber and Robyn Freedman Spitzman (1997).

Respite care
The family needs a lot of respite care to prevent them from burning out.

Enroute drug assistance:
Drugs are secondary to all the above mentioned strategies and drug therapy is always secondary to the environmentally friendly conditions with which we try to surround the FAS/E child. (Dosages are per the British Columbia Children's Hospital *Pediatric Drug Dosage Handbook*.)

For sleep disorders:	Mellaril
	Clonidine
	Melatonin
For ADHD:	Ritalin
	Dexadrine
	Clonidine
	Mellaril
	Paxil
For depression:	Prozac
	Zoloft
For OCD, ADHD and anxiety:	Paxil
	Prozac
For conduct disorder:	Occasionally Mellaril
For Tourette's Syndrome:	Clonidine
	Resperidal
For nutrition supplements:	Multi-vitamins
	Pediasure
	Ensure

You and your FAS/E children and families are likely to be journeying together for a long time. So a sense of humour, love and hope are an invaluable commodity for all concerned. Bon voyage!

3

The Role of Psychological Tests in FAS/E

Robert J. Williams

"Psychological tests" are instruments used in the assessment of personality, psychopathology, vocational interests, intellect, academic achievement, central nervous system (CNS) functioning, family functioning and child development. In some areas (e.g., intelligence, academic achievement and child development), they are the primary basis of assessment. In other areas (e.g., psychopathology and family functioning), they serve as secondary tools to supplement behavioural observations and/or a clinical interviews. Some instruments are self-report forms, some are third-party reports, some are time-limited tests, some are structured interviews and some are procedures for quantifying observed behaviour. There are thousands of psychometric instruments in existence. They are distinguished from each other by their reliability, validity and comprehensiveness. *Reliability* refers to the consistency and stability of the obtained scores. *Validity* concerns whether the test actually measures what it is intended to measure.

Test publishers have adopted the guidelines set forth in *Standards for Educational and Psychological Testing* (AERA, APA and NCME 1985) in determining who can administer and interpret tests. Some tests take considerable skill to administer and interpret and are restricted to individuals with at least a master's degree in psychology and specific training in the particular test ("level C tests"). Other tests are less complex and only require completion of a university course in psychometric assessment and some supervised experience in administering, scoring and interpreting tests ("level B tests"). Finally, some tests are simple to administer and interpret and can be used by anyone familiar with the test manual ("level A tests").

The assessment of fetal alcohol syndrome (FAS) is made when there is evidence of alcohol use during pregnancy, growth deficiencies, characteristic facial features, and central nervous system dysfunction. Psychological tests have two main roles with respect to FAS. The first is helping in the assessment of CNS dysfunction by measuring a child's functional capabilities. Functional skill assessment is particularly useful for detecting fetal alcohol effects (FAE) because CNS impairment can and usually does occur in the absence of growth, physical, or facial abnormalities (Clarren, Bowden and Astley 1985). The second main role of psychological tests is in helping to identify a person's pattern of strengths and weaknesses for treatment planning and prognosis.

Developmental Tests

Developmental tests assess the level of a child's behaviour in various domains compared to other children of the same age. Most of the better tests are a combination of interactive testing of the child and caregiver reports of the child's abilities. There is no agreed-upon categorization of developmental areas, but the following are most often used: motor skills (gross and fine), social/emotional skills, self-help skills, language skills (receptive and expressive) and sometimes visual-spatial skills or general cognitive skills. Most tests report developmental levels in each skill area as well as an overall "developmental quotient" or "composite score." Age equivalents, percentiles and standard scores are also commonly given. The child's percentile refers to his or her skill level compared to children of the same age (e.g., a percentile of 5 indicates that 95/100 children of this age have better skills; a percentile of 70 means that only 30/100 children of this age have better skills). A percentile below 5 indicates a significant delay. The average standard score for children in each age range is 100. In other words, if you take a thousand children, half of them would score above 100 and half would score below 100, but the average would be 100. Sixty-eight percent would score between 85 and 115 (one standard deviation) and 96 percent would score between 70 and 130 (two standard deviations). A standard score below 75 is usually taken to indicate a significant delay.

Developmental tests have several uses. The first is in determining whether the child has a significant delay. If there is a delay, the results will also indicate whether the delay is global, suggestive of mental retardation, or specific, perhaps suggestive of cerebral palsy or a learning disability. In addition to diagnostic information, these results provide important information about a child's strengths and weaknesses that can be used for program planning and as a baseline to monitor natural progress or the impact of an intervention. Children with FAS typically have developmental delays, with specific deficits in speech (Church and Kaltenbach 1997), imitatio and the development of standing and walking (Jacobson et al. 1993).

One problem with developmental tests is their limited predictive validity. Results tend to be highly predictive in the short term (i.e., the next twelve months) but weakly predictive of long-term ability (McCall 1979). The reasons for this are not totally clear but likely have to do with the stage-like progression of young children's abilities and their natural proneness to developmental spurts and lags. There are a few exceptions to this. Severely delayed children often continue to have serious delays (VanderVeer and Schweid 1974). The second is that some specific skills do have predictive validity. For example, infant novelty responses and quickness of habituation at 3–7 months correlates significantly (r = .45) with IQ at ages 2–7 (Fagan 1984).

There are many different developmental tests and screens. Based on reliability, validity and comprehensiveness (in terms of age range and abilities assessed), the best ones currently are the Bayley Scales of Infant Development II, the Battelle Developmental Inventory, and the Vineland Adaptive Behaviour Scales (see the Vineland, under "Adaptive Behaviour Tests").

Test	Year	Age	Level	Time	Categories and Forms
Bayley II	1993	0–3.5	C	25–60 min.	• Mental, motor, behaviour • 15 min. screening test also available
Battelle Developmental Inventory	1984	0–8	B	1–2 hr.	• Personal-social, adaptive, motor, communication, cognitive • 10–30 min. screening test available

Many other tests are limited, either because they assess a narrower age range (e.g., Miller Assessment for Preschoolers; Cognitive Ability Scales), have out-of-date norms (e.g., Cattelle Intelligence Tests for Infants and Young Children; Gesell Developmental Schedules; Minnesota Child Development Inventory) or have poor or unknown reliability and validity (e.g., Brigance Inventory of Early Development—Revised). It should be noted that common use of a test is no guarantee of its reliability and validity. One of the most frequently used screening tests has been the Denver Developmental Screening Test, which has a marked false negative bias (e.g., it often misses delays) (Burke et al. 1985; Harper and Wacker 1983), although this problem may have been corrected with the introduction of the Denver II (Frankenburg et al. 1992).

Adaptive Behaviour Tests

Tests of adaptive behaviour measure the person's functional levels in various life skills. Adaptive behaviour comprises independent functioning (e.g., feeding, cooking, dressing, toileting, hygiene, travelling, health care, money management, shopping, etc.); social functioning (e.g., communication skills, social interaction skills, sexual behaviour, child care);

and school or vocational functioning (e.g., reliability, performance, safety) (Demchak and Drinkwater 1993). Adaptive behaviour tests can be applied to both children and adults. Developmental tests are primarily a type of adaptive behaviour test that focuses on the functional behaviour of young children. Like developmental tests, tests of adaptive behaviour are typically combinations of third-party reports of a person's abilities and interactive tests of the individual.

Tests of adaptive behaviour determine whether the person has a delay, and whether the delay is global or specific. This in turn is useful for program planning and for establishing a baseline for intervention. In adults, tests of adaptive behaviour are also very useful in assessing the person's potential for living independently and/or the degree and nature of supports required for this to happen. Tests of adaptive behaviour are also useful for diagnostic purposes, as a diagnosis of mental retardation requires evidence of intellectual impairment along with significant impairment in adaptive behaviour. Indeed, tests of adaptive behaviour are the primary means of assessing severe levels (developmental skills in the 4–5-year range) and profound levels of retardation in adults (developmental skills in the 3-year or less range), because most intelligence tests do not test this low.

There are dozens of tests of adaptive behaviour. However, most have either a narrow focus (i.e., just assess severe and profound mental retardation, just children, just adults, etc.), have poor reliability and validity, out-of-date norms (e.g., the Adaptive Functioning Index) or do not use multiple sources of information in the assessment (i.e., direct observation plus caregiver reports). Based on reliability, validity and comprehensiveness, the best tests currently available are the Vineland Adaptive Behaviour Scales and the Scales of Independent Behaviour—Revised (SIB-R). The Vineland is better for developmental assessments, assessments of severe and profound retardation, assessments of older/higher functioning individuals and for making explicit distinctions between receptive and expressive language and gross and fine motor skills. The Scales of Independent Behaviour is superior to the Vineland in the assessment of vocational skills, money/property management and higher-level motor skills.

Test	Year	Age	Level	Time	Categories and Forms
Scales of Independent Behaviour— Revised	1994	0 to adult	B	40–50 min.	• Social and communication skills, personal living skills, community living skills, motor skills, problem behaviours • Screening test available

Vineland Adaptive Behaviour Scales	1984	0–19	B	20–90 min.	• Communication, daily living skills, socialization, motor skills, composite • Short survey form, long expanded form and classroom form

Intelligence Tests

Intelligence is the ability to adapt to one's environment. Successful adaptation requires capacity for learning, planning, abstract reasoning, application of prior learning, and the integrated coordination and use of component skills. Statistical techniques such as factor analysis have determined that intellectual skills are highly intercorrelated and that a general ability factor, called "g," accounts for most of the variance (Brody 1992; Sattler 1988). The main subcomponent skills are verbal/linguistic and visual-spatial abilities. Crystallized skills dependent on experience (e.g., knowledge/verbal skills) and fluid skills independent of experience (e.g., reasoning/spatial skills) is another valid dimensionalization (Brody 1992; Sattler 1988). Test score results are commonly reported in terms of standard scores or "Intelligence Quotients" (IQs), with the average standard IQ being 100 with a standard deviation of 15 or 16.

Intelligence tests have several uses. One is for diagnostic purposes. If a child is having difficulties in school, they can help determine whether this results from general intellectual slowness or some other problem (e.g., learning disability, attentional problem or lack of effort). Mental retardation is defined as having an overall IQ of two or more standard deviations below 100 (i.e., 68–70), along with significant impairments in adaptive functioning. A learning disability is defined as having a significant discrepancy between general intellectual ability and academic achievement in one particular area that is not due to lack of effort, opportunity or other environmental factors. Because of their diagnostic value, intellectual tests are those most commonly used to determine eligibility for special education funding in the schools. Learning disabilities and mental retardation are common amongst children with FAS. The average IQ of children with FAS is in the range of 60–70 (Conner and Streissguth 1996).

Like other tests, intellectual tests are also very useful for determining an individual's strengths and weaknesses for program planning. They are less useful in providing a baseline for intervention. After about age 6, intellectual ability tends to be fairly stable (Bloom 1964; Brody 1992). Because of the relative stability of IQ, intellectual ability has good predictive validity. Intellect is one of the best predictors of academic achievement, correlating between 0.4–0.6 with high school and college grades and educational attainment (McCall 1977). IQs are also one of the best

predictors of occupational attainment, unemployment and job performance, with correlations of 0.2–0.5 (Herrnstein and Murray 1994; Matarazzo
1972; Schmidt and Ones 1992).

Intelligence tests have some problems and limitations. First, because
they are interactive tests, accurate results are dependent upon cooperation, persistence and the absence of linguistic or perceptual (e.g., hearing
or vision) barriers. Second, there are some important cross-cultural problems in their application and interpretation (see "Special Population Considerations" below). Finally, although they capture much of what we think
of as intelligence, they also miss important areas such as creativity, social
skills, long-term problem solving, learning capability and "wisdom."

The intelligence tests currently having the best reliability and validity
are the Stanford-Binet Intelligence Scale (fourth edition), the Wechsler
Intelligence Scale for Children—III (WISC-III) and the Wechsler Adult
Intelligence Scale—Revised (WAIS-R) (the WAIS-III will replace the WAIS-
R when it is released):

Test	Year	Age	Level	Time	Categories and Forms
Stanford-Binet Intelligence Scale (4th edition)	1986	2 to adult	C	1–2 hrs.	• Verbal reasoning, abstract/visual reasoning, quantitative reasoning, short-term memory, composite score (factor-based scales also available)
WISC-III	1992	6–17	C	1 hr.	• Verbal IQ, performance IQ, full scale IQ (factor-based scales also available)
WAIS-R	1981	16 to adult	C	1 hr.	• Verbal IQ, performance IQ, full scale IQ

Other tests have limited use in intellectual assessment either because
(1) they include "nonintellectual" skills such as motor skills, musical
ability, etc. (e.g., Gardner's multiple intelligences, General Aptitude Test
Battery), (2) their construct validity is questionable (e.g., Kaufmann Assessment Battery for Children), (3) they have old norms (e.g., McCarthy
Scales of Children's Ability), (4) they have poor reliability or validity
(Leiter International Performance Scale, Black Intelligence Test of Cultural Homogeneity, Culture Fair Intelligence Test) or (5) they are too
restrictive in their focus (Peabody Picture Vocabulary Test, Raven Pro-

gressive Matrices). Some tests with good face validity (Learning Potential Assessment Device, Piagetian Scales) are limited by their lower reliability and no higher predictive validity.

Academic Achievement Tests

Academic achievement tests typically measure a person's grade and age levels in basic educational skills (reading, writing and arithmetic). These are interactive tests commonly administered by resource teachers in the school system. Like other tests, they are useful in providing an objective measure of a person's skills for program planning, to determine a person's strengths and weaknesses, to monitor progress and as a baseline to measure the impact of an intervention. Academic tests are also useful diagnostically, as the assessment of a learning disability requires a significant discrepancy between general intellectual ability and achievement in a specific area. FAS children commonly have lower educational attainment, particularly in math and some of the skills that underlie reading (Becker, Warr-Leeper and Leeper 1990; Streissguth et al. 1994).

There are many excellent academic achievement tests available (e.g., Kaufman Test of Educational Achievement, Metropolitan Achievement Tests, Peabody Individual Achievement Test—Revised, Diagnostic Achievement Battery—2). However, those with the greatest utility are the few that have been co-developed and co-normed with intellectual tests and thus allow direct comparison of the ability-achievement discrepancy. The two tests with this feature are the Wechsler Individual Achievement Test (WIAT) and the Woodcock-Johnson Psycho-Educational Battery—Revised (Tests of Achievement) (WJ-R-A).

Test	Year	Age	Level	Time	Categories and Forms
WIAT	1992	5–19	B	30–75 min.	• Reading, mathematics, writing, language, total composite • Screening test also available
WJ-R-A	1989	2–75	B	30 min. to 3 hrs.	• Oral language, reading, mathematics, written language, knowledge • Screening test also available

The Role of Psychological Tests in FAS/E

Neuropsychological Tests

Neuropsychological testing attempts to comprehensively assess all basic CNS skills (i.e., perceptual skills, visual-spatial skills, linguistic skills, mathematical skills, social-emotional skills, motor skills, memory and attention). It can be contrasted with intellectual assessment which is focused more on the assessment of higher-order, integrated CNS skills. Neuropsychological tests are interactive tests usually administered by psychologists, often with a specialty in neuropsychology. These tests can be useful in isolating the specific deficit underlying cognitive problems. The pattern of functional deficits is also sometimes used in assessing the presence or absence of neurological injury or disease, as well as localizing the site. Deficits in attention (Nanson and Hiscock 1990), visual-spatial memory (Uecker and Nadel 1996), verbal learning (Mattson et al. 1996) and visual-motor integration (Janzen, Nanson and Block 1995) have been reported in FAS children.

The traditional neuropsychological test batteries have been the Halstead-Reitan Battery and the Luria-Nebraska Neuropsychological Battery (Children's Revision). However, the reliability and validity of the Luria-Nebraska is questionable, and the Halstead-Reitan also has some weaknesses (Lezak 1995). Because of this, it is common for neuropsychologists to use a collection of individual tests to create their own battery. The main drawbacks to neuropsychological testing are the specialized expertise required in administration of the tests and the length of the assessment. Comprehensive neuropsychological testing typically takes several hours.

Psychological/Psychiatric Tests

The categorization of mental health problems has two main traditions. The first is the psychiatric tradition, which has identified syndromes of psychopathology based on clinical experience. This categorization is continually refined through successive editions of the *Diagnostic and Statistical Manual of Mental Disorders* (DSM-IV being the current edition). The second approach is more closely identified with psychology and is more empirical in nature. Here, categorizations of psychopathology are derived from statistical methods such as factor analysis that identify highly intercorrelated clusters. Some "psychological tests" provide scores on empirically derived factors (e.g., Child Behaviour Checklist), whereas others provide scores on predetermined clinical syndromes (e.g., Minnesota Multiphasic Personality Inventory, Behavior Dimensions Scale).

Like all standardized tests, psychological tests are useful in determining a person's level of behaviour compared to his or her peers. This is useful in determining the nature and seriousness of the problem. This in turn is useful diagnostically, for program planning and for establishing a baseline for intervention (e.g., evaluating the effectiveness of a behavioural program or stimulant medication). Hyperactivity, behavioural problems and deficits in self-regulation are commonly reported in FAS (Conner and Streissguth 1996; Kodituwakku et al. 1995).

The best tests are the ones that use multiple sources of information (i.e., have a self-report version, parent version or teacher version) and are comprehensive measures of psychopathology to allow comparisons between various areas. The Child Behaviour Checklist is probably the best test of this type for children, although there are several other good ones, including the Conners Rating Scales and the Behaviour Dimensions Scale. Despite their popularity, projective tests such as the Rorschach Ink Blot and Thematic Apperception Test have poor reliability and validity (Anastasi 1988). Projective techniques are best used as stimuli to supplement a clinical interview.

Test	Year	Age	Level	Time	Categories and Forms
Child Behavior Checklist	1991 –94	2–18	A	30–40 min.	• Withdrawn, somatic complaints, anxious/ depressed, social problems, thought problems, attention problems, delinquent behaviour, aggressive behaviour • Youth self-report (11–18), parent report (2–18), teacher report (5–18), direct observation form (5–14), semi-structured clinical interview (6–18)
Conners Rating Scale–Revised	1997	3–17	B	10–40 min.	• Oppositional, cognitive problems, hyperactivity, psychosomatic, anxious-shy, perfectionism, social problems, DSM-IV symptom subscales • Parent version, teacher version, self-report version, long and short forms

Behavior Dimensions Scale	1995	5–18	B	20–25 min.	• ADHD, oppositional-defiant, conduct disorder, avoidant personality, anxiety, depression • School version and home version

Special Population Considerations

Perceptual or Motor Handicaps

Special problems occur in the interactive testing of individuals with perceptual or motor impediments. Two approaches have been taken to this. The first has been the development of specialized tests that do not test or rely on skills that are weak (e.g., Hays-Binet for the blind, Hiskey-Nebraska Test of Learning Aptitude for the deaf). The second approach has been to use subtests from commonly used instruments such as the Wechsler (i.e., nonmotor subtests for individuals with motor impediments, verbal subtests for the blind, nonverbal tests for the deaf). Neither approach is totally satisfactory, as neither gives a comprehensive picture of the person's abilities. However, of the two approaches, the latter one is recommended, as the validity of the specialized instruments is not as good as that of the mainstream instruments (Sattler 1988). Clinician unfamiliarity with their administration may further compromise validity.

A second problem concerns which norms to use. Certain tests (e.g., Vineland) report separate norms for various handicaps (e.g., mental, physical, visual, hearing) in addition to the regular norms. Both norms are informative, as one provides the person's standing relative to others with the same handicap, and the other provides the person's standing relative to the general population.

Language Problems

A test bias exists for individuals who do not have English as a first language (e.g., Valencia and Rankin 1988). Administering nonverbal subtests from mainstream instruments is a partial solution but again does not provide a comprehensive picture of the person's abilities. If test items are translated, distortion can occur in the translation of the question and the interpretation of the person's answers. This risk is reduced when the translator is familiar with the test and routinely provides translation for it. When possible, the best procedure is to administer a test that is available in the person's first language. Unfortunately, very few of the above-mentioned tests are available in languages other than English (Stanford-Binet in French, WISC-R in Spanish).

Different Cultures

There are well established ethnic/racial differences in psychological test results. For example, in the developmental area, Aboriginal children tend to have weaker verbal abilities than Caucasian children (Blanchard 1983). Asian infants tend to be lower in motor activity, irritability and vocalization compared to Caucasian infants (Kagan, Arcus and Snidman 1993). In the area of intellectual ability, African Americans and Aboriginals tend to score lower than Caucasians on IQ tests (just verbal sections for Aboriginals), and east Asians somewhat higher (primarily in the visual-spatial sections) (Iwawaki and Vernon 1988; Lynn 1991; McShane and Berry 1988; Vernon, Jackson and Messick 1988). The area of academic achievement tends to parallel IQ results, with higher levels of achievement in mathematics and science for students from east Asian countries and lower general achievement for African Americans, Hispanics and Aboriginals (McShane and Berry 1988; National Center for Education Statistics 1991; Sue and Okazaki 1990). In the psychiatric/psychological area, the overall prevalence of psychopathology in North America tends to be higher in African Americans, Aboriginals and Hispanics (Bulhan 1985; Cuellar and Roberts 1984; LaFromboise 1988).

These results are not in dispute. What is in dispute is their meaning. The first thing to realize is that there is no absolute standard for comparison. Is it that Aboriginal children are verbally delayed or Caucasian children verbally advanced? Are minority children more behaviourally disordered or majority children overly socialized? The second thing to realize is that the origin for virtually all these tests is the United States. Thus, not only are the norms North American, but also the definitions and measurement of "development," "intelligence," "achievement," and "psychopathology" tend to have a White Western bias.

The recognition of cultural relativity has led to the development of more "culture-neutral" versions of these instruments in recent years. However, more culturally neutral intelligence tests have not eliminated most of the original cultural/racial differences that existed. This is because the differences (except for Aboriginals) are actually wider on more culturally neutral visual-spatial items than on culturally loaded verbal items (Jensen and McGurk 1987).

There can never truly be a "culture-free" psychological test, as the relative importance of skills and behaviours is often different between cultures. Some of the skills measured in traditional intelligence tests (e.g., speed, verbal ability, mathematic ability, abstract analysis) are less important for some cultures than skills not directly assessed (e.g., social skills, practical problem solving, auditory/olfactory/kinesthetic awareness). The interpretation of behaviour can also be different. From my own experience in northern Manitoba, I recall a case where a child was biting other children and growling like a wolf. His school was quite upset because this behaviour was very strange and disruptive, whereas his father was quite proud, as he was a member of the wolf clan and believed his son was imbued with the spirit of the wolf. The pathological interpretation of boisterous behaviour differs between Eastern and Western cultures (Mann et al. 1992; Weisz et al. 1987). Finally, things sometimes manifest themselves differently between cultures. Psychosomatic manifestations of distress are more common in developing countries (American Psychiatric Association 1994). Amongst the Aboriginal population, it is not uncommon for depression to take the form of a loss or disturbed sense of spirituality, connection with ancestors and/or connection with the Creator (see also Shore and Manson 1981; Timpson et al. 1988).

However, this does not mean that psychological test results are totally invalid for cultures that are not White Western in origin, as there is also good evidence of the cross-cultural existence of developmental stages (Dasen 1977), major intellectual factors (Hennessy and Merrifield 1976) and major forms of psychopathology (WHO 1973, 1983 and 1992). Furthermore, some of the differences are due to biological compromises rather than cultural emphasis. Aboriginal children have significantly higher rates of middle-ear disease, visual problems, fetal alcohol exposure, lead exposure and poor nutrition that would impair development and ability in any culture (Burd and Moffatt 1994; May 1988). Finally, the predictive validity of psychological tests in North American society is roughly the same for all cultures, e.g., IQ predicts school and job performance equally well for all cultural/racial groups (Breland 1979; Schmidt and Ones 1992).

To summarize, ethnic/racial differences in psychological test results represent true differences in abilities and behaviours that reflect primarily White Western conceptualizations of intelligence, development, achievement and mental health. As such, test results are quite useful as good predictors of success and adaptation to mainstream North American society for any individual or ethnic/racial group. However, psychological tests tend to be less valid as absolute measures of intelligence, development or mental health for non-White, non-Western individuals, as different cultures have somewhat different meanings for these concepts. As a consequence, they are also probably somewhat less predictive of success in non-White, non-Western cultures. Thus, psychological tests have potential utility for all individuals, but the above considerations must be taken into account when interpreting and communicating test results for individuals from different cultures.

4

The Role of the Community Health Nurse in Dealing with FAS/E

Joanne Alexander and Pat Short

The delivery room is filled with excitement and activity as preparations are made to welcome a new life into the world. With one final push, a 3120-gram baby girl emerges with a lusty cry. This delivery is like any other, except for one thing: this mother drank alcohol during her pregnancy. All newborns require community health nurse support, but it is especially critical when a child has fetal alcohol syndrome (FAS) or fetal alcohol effects (FAE).

The role of the community health nurse is encompassed in the broad objective of ensuring that every child is born with the best possible start, thus enabling them to develop to their fullest potential. The community health nurse works toward enabling people to help themselves in the best way possible. Out of necessity, this means engaging a much larger group than the mother and child. It takes a community to raise a child, and healthy children require healthy communities. The objectives of building a healthy community can be met for every child. This does not mean that everyone will have perfect babies in perfect situations. Striving for perfection is unrealistic and unachievable. However, the experienced community health nurse has learned that making small changes while achieving small goals on many different levels can have far-reaching effects.

Here we will look at community and family issues the community health nurse can address. The strategies used for community and family are interrelated, but they will be distinguished for the purpose of discussion. The term *community* is multifaceted, referring to family, friends, school, workplace and the community at large. A change in one impacts on the others.

Focus on the Community: Community Health Nursing Strategies for Education and Prevention of FAS/E

The goal sounds simple: educate communities about the effects of alcohol during pregnancy in order to stop pregnant women from drinking. Many avenues have already been used effectively: public policy, advertising, school systems, community workshops, open forums and prenatal education. These methods of education represent a beginning toward increasing awareness about the effects of alcohol use in pregnancy. Women do not usually start drinking alcohol when they become pregnant. This behaviour usually starts long before conception, but knowledge does not always change behaviour.

A community profile needs to be assembled in order to develop effective educational strategies. Good profiles are built by asking the right questions. Some questions that may be helpful when developing a profile are:

1. *Is the community aware that a problem exists?* What is the rate of alcohol consumption? How much liquor is sold locally? What are the rates of alcohol-related accidents and crimes? How many people suffer from alcohol-related disease? How many children are diagnosed FAS/E? What percentage of pregnant women drink alcohol? How many seek counseling to decrease alcohol intake? What role does alcohol play at the time of conception?

2. *Does the community recognize the full extent and impact of FAS/E?* What percentage of the following people were exposed to alcohol prenatally: failure-to-thrive infants; children who are abused; children in foster care; adults experiencing difficulty in school; people involved in crime; prison inmates; role models; or the elderly? What percentage of service dollars are spent on FAS/E? How available are local statistics? Are they presented to the community? How willing are community members to take responsibility for the prevention of FAS/E?

3. *What is the community attitude toward pregnant women?* What cultural values are present? What is available to nurture and support pregnant women? Do women deny pregnancy? If so, why? Are alcohol-free drinks readily available? If so, what are their quality? What attitudes do alcohol-free women face? How are women who are trying to avoid alcohol supported? What resources are available? How accessible are they to all women?

4. *When do women drink?* At what age do they start? Who do they most often drink with? How often is alcohol part of celebrations, holidays, sports? Do women drink more in early or late pregnancy? How comfortable are they admitting their drinking patterns? What roles do their friends, family and partner play?

5. *Why do women drink?* Ask women of all ages. Do alcohol counselors record reasons? If so, what are they? Has any research been done? Is it easier to drink or not drink? Why? Do women hide or deny the pregnancy so they can drink without pressure or guilt? How many nondrinking women does the drinking woman know? What role do these women play in her life?

6. *Who are the role models and what are they demonstrating?* Who

are the community role models? What is their behaviour? How closely are they observed or used as an example? Who are the people with power and control? Do these people exert a positive or negative influence? Who influences the role models?

The community health nurse, in cooperation with other community members, could play a role in addressing any or all of these questions. Community health nurses become skilled at recognizing strengths within a community, seeking out appropriate people who have a high community profile and utilizing these individuals for effective strategic planning.

The community health nurse brings to the multidisciplinary team a holistic and valuable perspective, as she or he interacts with clients in all aspects of their lives, including where they live, work, play and learn. Client caseloads include a full spectrum of the community, from those who struggle to meet their most basic needs to those who meet their needs with ease and abundance. This puts the community health nurse in a position to observe strengths and weaknesses both within the community and among individuals. It is important to recognize that a community and its members cannot be dissected, but they function together as a whole. Focus is not only on the individual but also on the community that surrounds that person, including family, partners, children, teachers, role models and the community at large. Similarly, the community functions as a whole, being more than the sum of its members. The two strongly influence one another. Change in one will impact the other. Participating and assisting a community and its members to make changes in the same direction can be inspiring and exciting. Communities as a whole must learn to recognize that women who feel loved, supported, secure and respected are unlikely to drink while pregnant.

Focus on Families: Community Health Nurse Strategies for Working with Families in Prevention of FAS/E

Community health nurses work with individuals and families from throughout the entire lifespan. Quite often, first contact with a family surrounds the birth of a child. Nurses play an important role in providing a variety of services to a family, including support, education, advocacy, coordination of a multidisciplinary team and facilitation toward change. Families provide nurses with an opportunity to work with people of all ages, both in prevention of alcohol-related birth defects and establishment of relationships with those affected by FAS/E.

The prevention goal is similar to the community goal but no less simple: teach women that drinking alcohol while pregnant can harm the unborn baby and stop women from drinking alcohol while pregnant. Ideally, prevention should begin at least three months prior to conception, but, in reality, opportunity for contact often does not arise until the second trimester.

The Role of the Community Health Nurse

Knowing and seeing the devastating effects that alcohol use in pregnancy can have on a person's life makes this a unique and challenging area of work. It presents us with an opportunity to examine our own values and look at how effective we can be in these situations. Some questions the community health nurse needs to ask himself or herself are: How do I feel about women who drink while pregnant? How effectively can I work with this person to facilitate positive change? Can I accept this person and her circumstances for what they are?

One of the most difficult challenges in working with pregnant women who drink is to accept them and not pass judgment on their behaviour. It is important to recognize the positive aspects of individual situations and build on those, no matter how small. The goal is to assist the mother to make as many changes as possible for the improved health of the infant. If alcohol cannot be eliminated at this time, it can often be reduced. Meanwhile, improving nutrition, decreasing stress levels, exploring options for coping and reducing other drug use, including cigarettes, can further aid the harm-reduction process. The community health nurse needs to recognize and accept the limitations of a given situation, while making appropriate referrals and coordinating services to best meet the needs of individual clients and their families.

In a society where alcohol is both widely accepted and readily available, its use often begins long before the pregnancy. The reasons women continue to drink while pregnant are as varied and individual as there are people. Therefore it is important to look at some of the reasons why this occurs. It is easy to sit in judgment of others or to simplify the situation by saying, "She should know better" or "All she has to do is quit," when in reality there are many factors involved. Past history may involve violence including sexual, physical or emotional abuse, which result in low self-esteem and rob the body of spirit. Often the onus for a healthy pregnancy outcome is put solely upon the woman, which is sometimes a heavy burden to carry. Without the support of partner, family, friends and members of the larger community, this responsibility can be overwhelming. Depending on age, marital status, partner's work schedule and association with the community, women who are pregnant may find themselves isolated and alone. They may also be solely responsible for the care of other children and the home, which can lead to high stress levels.

Some questions that may need to be answered are: Why is this woman drinking? What stage of the pregnancy is she in? What are the circumstances surrounding this pregnancy? What are her strengths? What are her coping mechanisms? What changes has she made already? How willing is she to make additional changes?

Case planning needs to be flexible to meet the needs of each client. In order to facilitate effective changes in behaviour, intervention needs to continue beyond delivery. Continued intervention may mean assistance with parenting skills, as well as working toward increasing positive outcomes for subsequent pregnancies.

When developing strategies for prevention, the community health nurse should address a number of quesions: How will you obtain referrals? What are some ways to obtain referrals earlier? How will I make contact with women? Who are the members of my team? How can this woman's needs best be met—individual counseling, support groups, prenatal classes? What resources are available? How aware of these is the woman? What service can I best provide? What is the community's network and how can I use it? How and when will I refer to other agencies?

After the birth of a child, community health nurse contact is often made with the mother while she is still in hospital. This is an opportunity to establish the framework for an ongoing relationship with mother, infant and family that involves education, advocacy and support. One of the biggest tasks is to assist in empowering the family, reassuring them that they know themselves and their child best. It is important for them to know and understand they have choices and are capable of making decisions. The community health nurse will continue her role as educator, advocate and prevention worker.

Small Northern Communities

Small, northern and often isolated communities bring a uniqueness that can provide the community health nurse with rewarding and challenging options. Opportunity arises for the community health nurse to be instrumental in directing community change. Based on our experience, this can happen more readily in small northern communities for many reasons:

- Service providers are usually smaller in number, yet more visible in the community, which allows for easier coordination and strategic planning.
- Committees are easy to establish and come together readily.
- There is greater opportunity to be creative and pioneer new ideas.
- Local governing bodies are more accessible and approachable.
- Committed individuals are often instrumental in facilitating great change.
- Community members have close ties to the community and are often dedicated to working together for change.
- It is easier to mobilize an entire community when it is small and isolated.
- Word travels quickly through an integrated network.

The Role of the Community Health Nurse

A great deal of prevention and education in the area of FAS/E has been carried out in the North, but lack of follow-up research has made it difficult to determine if this has been instrumental in creating positive change.

In the field of community health and health education, change is often slow. This role can be challenging and frustrating, especially in a society geared toward immediate results. At present we strive for the healthiest baby in the healthiest situation possible. It is our hope that through the continued efforts of committed people, FAS/E will be eliminated in future generations.

· 5 ·

FAS and FAE in Classrooms: Strategies for Educators

Anne Lindsay and Donna Preston

In this chapter we will discuss strategies for dealing with fetal alcohol children in schools. Much of the resource material developed to date has been aimed at teachers. However, as discussed here, strategies for dealing with children with fetal alcohol syndrome or fetal alcohol effects (FAS/E) must include a broader audience, and we will be considering strategies for educators generally. First the incidence of FAS/E is discussed, followed by features particularly relevant to classroom functioning, and issues of identification and assessment. We then discuss strategies that school systems can adopt to help address FAS/E. Finally, we consider implications of northern educational contexts for interventions with FAS/E. Our discussion is based on various sources, and also on our own work in a grade one classroom with one formally diagnosed FAS child and a number of others suspected of having FAE.

Incidence of FAS/E

Currently the incidence of FAS is estimated to be 1–3 per 1,000 births in North America (Burgess and Streissguth 1992) and the incidence of FAE about 1 in 300–350. Given these figures, one would expect approximately one case of FAS or FAE in a school of 225. However, as Burgess and Streissguth (1992: 46) argued:

> These statistics are probably very conservative in that they reflect only those children who have actually been identified, referred and diagnosed with these conditions. Considering the number of young people who may be affected but remain unrecognized, we can only assume that FAS and FAE are problems that have a significant impact on our social and environmental services.

Furthermore, this incidence can vary according to community. In particular, it may be more prevalent in northern communities where there has been a history of higher rates of alcohol and drug abuse (Schmidt and Turpin 1996). It follows that cases of FAS or FAE can be expected in northern schools.

Strategies for Educators

The Academic Profile

A cluster of physical and intellectual features are associated with FAS/E. Damage to the central nervous system caused by maternal alcohol consumption during pregnancy often results in the intellectual impairment of a child. FAS is now considered to be the leading known cause of mental retardation in Western countries (Burgess and Streissguth 1992). Although there is considerable variation in IQ among these children, scores are typically below normal, averaging 65–70, with a range of 30–105 for FAS and a slightly higher average but the same range for FAE (Burgess and Streissguth 1992). Learning is often slower, with difficulties in processing information, abstract thought, and cause and effect reasoning. Poor judgment is common among these children and leads to difficulty in differentiating right from wrong and understanding the consequences of actions.

A second cluster of features involves global attentional factors which affect all aspects of a child's functioning in school. These have been described in considerable detail in various fetal alcohol studies (e.g., Burgess and Streissguth 1992; Smitherman 1994). Typically, FAS/E children are described as hyperactive, distractible and impulsive, with high activity levels. These features might all be thought of as part of a more general attentional problem. As Nanson and Hiscock (1996: 33) explain, these children have "difficulty with the investment, organization and maintenance of attention over time."

Another set of features involves sociolinguistic skills. In contrast to conventional notions of language which focus on articulation, vocabulary or sentence structure, these skills, often referred to as communication skills, involve the use of language in social contexts and so involve the intersection of social and linguistic knowledge. Children with FAS/E often have a superficial facility with language that disguises serious communication problems. As Burgess and Streissguth (1992) pointed out, for such children there may be a discrepancy between the level of verbal language as it appears on a test and the child's ability to use language in ongoing communication. For example, they may have difficulty understanding how to initiate or maintain a conversation (British Columbia 1996). Conversational skill requires knowing the rules for turn taking in different contexts, such as large-group versus one-to-one interaction. It also requires skill in topic development, such as staying on topic and understanding topic patterns such as causal versus temporal order. Such problems with participation in classroom interaction not only hinder children's opportunities for learning directly, but they also impact negatively on the development of peer relations which would support various aspects of classroom functioning.

Another feature typical of FAS/E children is a disruptive family life, frequently marked by the death of the biological mother and placement in foster care (Smitherman 1994), and foster placements may be multiple due to the difficulty experienced in caring for such children. Where children continue to live with the biological mother, the home is frequently characterized by ongoing alcohol abuse, neglect and other related effects.

In many special-needs syndromes, impairment is highly specific and often limited to one domain, with the possibility of compensation depending on strengths in other areas. FAS/E children suffer serious damage or risk across a variety of domains. Whereas impairment in any one domain may not appear as severe as with other disorders, it is the global nature of the damage that is so disabling. Not surprisingly, academic performance of FAS/E children is generally not expected to exceed a grade six to grade eight level. This academic profile indicates that effective intervention needs to be broad-based and begun early to maximize much-needed opportunities for learning for these children and to minimize or avoid the learning of inappropriate behaviours.

Identification and Assessment

Teachers with FAS/E children in the classroom see students who are often disruptive, demanding and academically underachieving. However, such children are unlikely to be identified as FAS/E. Instead, they are often labelled as behaviour problems and their academic difficulties are seen as an outcome. Fetal alcohol syndrome often goes undiagnosed and unrecognized even by physicians (Burgess and Streissguth 1992; Little et al. 1990). Although educational settings provide ample opportunity to observe the range of the behavioural and intellectual problems of such children, teachers often lack sufficient knowledge of FAS/E to suspect its presence (Finlay and Sorenson 1995).

Even if teachers do consider the possibility that a child's problems are fetal alcohol–related, formal testing and identification can be very difficult. As the diagnosis is medical, it cannot be made by educators. Furthermore, it requires evidence of prenatal alcohol intake, and so parental cooperation. It also involves the stigma of alcohol abuse. For some parents it is a relief to discover that the child's problems are not the fault of their parenting, but for others it is a sensitive and painful issue they would prefer to avoid. Consequently, many fetal alcohol children enter the school system with no formal diagnosis. They may then be recognized as potential cases and referred for medical assessment. However, many of these children are no longer with their biological mothers and the requisite information on prenatal alcohol use may be difficult to obtain, meaning a diagnosis cannot be made. Furthermore, when they are sent for testing within the school system, no particular problem may be identified. As Finlay and Sorenson (1995) point out, even when these children are recognized, they often slip through the cracks. Many are incorrectly labelled as learning disabled or attention deficit disordered, syndromes that do not cover the range of the educational needs of these children.

Strategies Beyond the Classroom Level

Given the academic prognosis of fetal alcohol–damaged children and the difficulties in their identification, teachers' knowledge of FAS/E is a crucial link in early intervention. Not only is knowledge critical for making referrals for formal assessment, but teachers may be left working with these children and their families in the absence of a formal diagnosis, supported only by their personal understanding of the problem. However, an expectation that classroom teachers alone can mitigate the numerous manifestations of this complex social issue is not only an unfair but also an often ineffectual strategy.

Given the above, three of the recommendations made by Burgess and Streissguth (1992) should be considered fundamental. They are aimed at improving the identification, assessment and understanding of fetal alcohol children, and all require action at the school district level. Burgess and Streissguth argued that it was essential that districts provide for the education of all school personnel about fetal alcohol syndrome. Clearly, teachers need to be knowledgeable about FAS/E. However, if principals and district-level administrators are going to provide the necessary aid for teachers, often without any formal support system, they will need to be convinced that the problems of particular children may be fetal alcohol–related. They will also need to understand the inherent issues. As well, paraprofessionals, specialists and parents need to be included in this training. We would further add that an understanding of fetal alcohol–affected children needs to become incorporated into teacher training programs. Information necessary for such training has accumulated in recent years. It has been well described in various sources (e.g., Burgess and Streissguth 1992; Finlay and Sorenson 1995; Schmidt and Turpin 1996) and is not discussed further here.

Burgess and Streissguth (1992) also stated that school districts need to develop strategies to improve identification of possible cases through interaction with routine health screening processes. They acknowledged the sensitivity of the underlying issues but argued that we should be able to find ways to deal with them. They recommended that referral systems for formal assessment of these cases need to be developed. As they stated, without this vital link, educators who have become knowledgeable about fetal alcohol damage may only become frustrated and perhaps discouraged in their intervention attempts.

Strategies at the School Level

Support for dealing with FAS/E must also come at the school level. The range of difficulties experienced by these children frequently requires consultation with a variety of specialists. Finlay and Sorenson (1995) argued that managing FAS/E children involves a collaborative teamwork approach. Not only does such an approach bring a range of resources into the educational planning for a child, but it builds in much-needed support for teachers and parents. However, unlike Finlay and Sorenson, we do not think that organization of such intervention teams should be the responsibility of the teacher. Strategies need to relieve pressure on the teacher in dealing with such cases. We recommend that school staff put intervention teams in place and then encourage teachers to consult them. The value of this approach was clearly apparent in the school where our observations were made. A school-based team was already established to advise on a broad range of classroom difficulties. It provided a way for the teacher to find not just advice but much-needed support.

Strategies at the Classroom Level

Given the difficulties with assessment and diagnosis, it is clear that teachers will continue to find themselves with FAS/E children in their classrooms with little or no aid. Even where a referral is made, they must work with these children in the often long interim before testing can be done. For children with a formal diagnosis, teachers play a key role in developing individual educational plans, implementing them and evaluating the child's progress. As well, in today's integrated classrooms, teachers work with all children across the many contexts of a school day. Understanding ways to adapt their teaching will not only benefit the child but also other children and the teacher.

Program Goals

Current philosophies of education hold that all children should have the same educational opportunities. This means that the goals of a school system should extend to all children, with adaptations on teaching approaches for children with special needs. As Burgess and Streissguth (1992) argued, a fundamental consideration in modification of educational plans should always be the original intent of the system's goals. For example, a common strategy with FAS/E children is to structure their activities tightly by eliminating flexibility and choice. However, as Burgess and Streissguth noted, this strategy would conflict with the goal to have students learn to take control of their own behaviour and so become independent. What needs to be recognized is that a modification which works towards accomplishing one goal may create a conflict with another.

The academic profile of FAS/E children indicates that goals specific to their needs must be articulated. In particular, these children need to have opportunities to learn functional skills. In many cases the curriculum needs to be broadened to include application of school-based learning skills to social and vocational settings, for example using literacy skills to fill out job applications (Burgess and Streissguth 1992). Other goals that need articulating include communication and social skills.

The Learning Environment

Understanding the attentional difficulties of these children and their problems with processing information has led to various suggestions for simplifying classroom functioning through the design of the learning environment. The major principles of this strategy are discussed by Osborne (1994). First, the classroom should include quiet zones where children can learn to retreat when they feel overstimulated. The classroom spaces and materials need to be carefully and consistently designed and clearly marked, including seating areas for particular activities, and rules for use of these areas and materials. In contrast to the atmosphere found in many classrooms, Osborne (1994) and others (e.g., British Columbia 1996) recommend a classroom design that minimizes distraction, a strategy which unfortunately may be difficult to reconcile with the needs and interests of other children using this space.

A number of sources concentrate on modifications of tasks within the classroom learning environment (e.g., British Columbia 1996; Lutke 1993; Osborne 1994). Typically such recommendations focus on the conceptual structure of the task. These include use of concrete and practical activities that relate to children's personal experience, such as math concepts presented with money. Another recommendation is to simplify and carefully sequence each task. Suggested strategies also provide ways to illustrate or clarify the conceptual structure to the child, such as by labelling, providing examples and using checklists. It is also typically recommended to provide more assistance, time, repetition, routine, consistency, feedback and evidence of success. Tasks should also require less reading, less copying and fewer choices. Multimodal and multisensory designs are also typically recommended. Recommendations also include adapting materials, for example, by reducing the reading level and by using calculators.

Classroom Interaction

It is our belief that no single strategy has more impact on children and their learning than the ways teachers organize the interaction and communication in their classrooms. Teachers accomplish this through the use of different groupings of children and by control of the communicative process. Given the FAS/E child's attentional and sociolinguistic difficulties, teacher communication is of particular significance. All discussions of FAS/E intervention make mention of teacher interaction or communication style (e.g., British Columbia 1996; Burgess and Streissguth 1992). Typical is the advice to emphasize nonverbal features of language to reinforce a verbal message, for example, by using gesture, facial expression, intonation, proximity or eye contact. The use of vocabulary appropriate to the child's level and avoidance of complex sentence structures and idiomatic and ambiguous phrasings are also advised.

The above suggestions address only the basic communicative elements used by teachers and not the broader issues involved in the social organization of communication. Education literature contains considerable research into classroom interaction patterns of teachers and children. These include studies of large-group interaction patterns (e.g., Erickson 1996), small group patterns (e.g., de la Cruz and Brandt 1995) and connections between classroom discourse and cognitive and social development (e.g., Cazden 1988; Hicks 1995; Pappas, Kiefer and Levstik 1995; Wells and Chang-Wells 1992). These studies document different ways of organizing interaction and how they impact children's classroom functioning and learning. Increasingly, interaction patterns are being understood to play a vital role in the teaching/learning process. However, they are not commonly included in discussions of FAS/E children in classrooms.

FAS/E Children in Large- and Small-Group Interaction.

We found the most supportive interaction pattern for FAS/E children to be a one-to-one, or dyadic, structure. However, much time in classrooms is spent on independent tasks, large-group teacher-led activity and various types of small-group activity. Many of the strategies suggested for adapting classroom practice for FAS/E children are modifications to independent tasks, for example, completing assigned work or tests. As noted above, large- and small-group interaction patterns have received little attention.

As would be expected given the attentional and sociolinguistic difficulties of FAS/E children, we found that large-group activity is not easily managed. Asking these children to sit still for too long is setting them up for failure. Withdrawing them to work with a teacher assistant is an obvious solution, but such assistance is not always available. Also, they need to learn to manage within these kinds of group situations. Through trial and error, we found some strategies that work. For example, giving the child a teddy bear to hold during a group time and having an alternative activity ready before the demands of the large-group activity become too great proved successful. However, in general, large-group functioning is an area that needs further attention, in particular given the high expectation for children to learn within this structure.

Similarly, little discussion seems to have taken place around the use of small-group activities. In the classroom where we were working, all children were encouraged to work collaboratively and to give and receive help from one another. A collaborative approach was modelled by the teacher and then supported by structuring children's activities to work interdependently. In our observations, peer interaction in informal small groups appeared to be an important support for the learning of the FAS/E children. Again, as with large-group activity, we think small-group activity needs more attention.

FAS/E Children during Transitions

In the classroom where we made our observations, the teacher used an individual educational plan for the identified FAS child and assigned teacher-aide time to him. As an experienced teacher, she drew on strategies for working with the child that had been successful with other children who were not FAS/E. However, these often proved unsuccessful. Careful observation of classroom activity suggested that major problems originated in the activity before, after and between tasks—during transitions. Transitions involved instructions for starting and carrying out tasks, and for changing tasks. They also included entry and exit routines. Some were teacher-initiated, but others were child-initiated. Grouping structures are a very visible aspect of the social organization of communication in classrooms. Transitions are the events that bridge the substantive classroom activities and may be seen as insignificant in contrast to the real work that goes on within activities. However, they form the essential medium within which all activity proceeds. Experienced teachers realize this when they spend extended periods of time and efforts establishing classroom routines and rules in the first weeks with a new class. If transitions do not function smoothly, the best-planned activities are adversely affected.

We suspected that the sociolinguistic problems and attentional difficulties of FAS/E children made them especially vulnerable to managing transitions throughout a day. We decided to observe them more closely and noticed that the teacher was using a distinctive interaction pattern in classroom transitions, giving general instructions to the whole group without focusing attention on herself. We observed that this strategy was effective with the other children but did not typically work with the FAS/E children, who had difficulty listening to and following her directions. Generally, the FAS/E children ignored her and continued their present activity. Upon further observation, we noted that a high proportion of the teacher's talk during transitions was directed at these children. We also observed that the FAS/E children did not seem to follow the lead of others in such events. Initially the teacher thought that the whole class was exhibiting similar behaviour, but gradually she came to realize that it was primarily the children she knew or suspected to have FAS/E.

Consulting a variety of sources, we found a number of suggestions (e.g., British Columbia 1996; Osborne 1994) which we summarized into an approach for handling transitions. For example, by establishing clear routines for exit and entry, and preparing children in advance for changes in routines, smoother operations were promoted. This cluster of modifications seemed to make a significant impact on the FAS/E children's ability to handle transitions. Our observations confirmed for us the frequency, importance and complexity of these events. We noted the need to plan specifically for the transitions as well as the substantive activities of the FAS/E children. We believe that this is an area of the classroom functioning of FAS/E children that needs further examination.

FAS/E Children and Control of the Communicative Process

Another aspect of teacher-child interaction is the general style of communication a teacher uses to conduct her or his class. One recommendation sometimes found is that teachers should use a directive style of teaching with FAS/E children. A directive style is characterized by interaction in which the teacher retains tight control over all aspects of classroom activity by giving clear directions which children are expected to follow with little or no question. It can be thought of as a one-way style of communication or interaction.

Although we recognize the simplicity of information processing in the directive approach, we have some reservations about its value. It is typically associated with a transmissional approach to teaching where teachers are assumed to have knowledge which they convey to children, who in turn passively absorb it. In contrast, other approaches assume that children need to be actively involved in their learning processes and that teaching needs to be interactive to be effective. Another reservation we have is that the low level of interactivity may also represent a low level of pedagogical bonding between teacher and child, a quality that may be significant for learning (Lindsay 1997).

In summary, while we agree with recommendations made elsewhere about the necessity of adapting communication styles with FAS/E children, we also think there are many important features of teacher-child interaction yet to be considered. At present, there is little information available on how communication patterns are constructed between teachers and FAS/E children and with what effects. Dealing with FAS/E children in our schools requires a broad-based approach with support at various levels. Adapting teaching practices is multifaceted and extends across and between all activities in the school day.

Strategies for Educators

The Northern Context

For a number of years the supply of teachers in Canada has far exceeded the demand. Many graduates from teacher training have come from urban environments in the South and wish to remain there, close to families and friends, and to retain their urban lifestyles. The reality has been that the only permanent, full-time jobs available have been in remote and northern settings. If these graduates wished to have a classroom of their own, they have had little choice but to move north. Life in these remote settings frequently means a more severe climate; fewer recreational opportunities; limited access to arts, sporting events, radio and television; diminished and different social activities; a spartan selection of stores and restaurants; a more limited and less interesting diet; and isolation from friends and families.

Schools in such communities typically lack many of the amenities of their larger urban counterparts. For example, there may be limited gym equipment, or no gym at all. Outdoor recreation opportunities and the variety of sites for field trips are limited, and libraries may be inadequate. Colleagues who otherwise might be supportive of young teachers in such settings may be struggling with the same challenges. Others with whom they are likely to socialize, such as nurses, social workers and police officers, face similar circumstances. For most teachers, the first years in a classroom are often the most challenging of their lives. Combined with the challenges of remote and northern positions, it is not surprising that many have preferred to stay in more familiar places.

Of the young teachers who have chosen such jobs, many have risen to the personal and professional challenges, even deciding to stay permanently in their adopted communities. However, for others, their time in such settings has always been temporary and frequently undesirable and unpleasant. The result is that northern communities have had difficulty recruiting teachers, as well as other professionals, to work with their children long-term (Schmidt and Turpin 1996). The professional and community contexts do not optimally support the development of teaching skills and the building of professional teams highly committed to the well-being of children and families. Frequently, after teachers have acquired some degree of expertise, they leave for more desirable locations.

Teachers generally lack knowledge about FAS/E. Teachers in northern contexts may also lack the commitment and support to help them develop such knowledge. However, as discussed above, dealing with FAS/E in schools does not just require a restructuring of particular activities but, rather, broad-based adaptation of teaching practices. And it also requires systemic support and commitment. Northern communities with a higher incidence of FAS/E are also less able to provide the comprehensive range of professional services that can help address the needs of the children,

71

families and communities. While there are no easy solutions, understanding the issues helps educators put the problems into perspective. Understanding also points to the importance of policy and intervention on a broader scale to address the educational issues of fetal alcohol damage, especially in the North.

Summary

The mandate of teachers in schools across Canada has grown out of proportion to their time and abilities to manage it. The challenges of teaching in northern communities and the incidence of FAS/E there place further demands on already strained teachers. It is crucial in making recommendations regarding problems in our schools that policymakers, professionals and the general public not be encouraged to think that the solution lies in extending the teachers' mandate and simply providing them with the relevant professional development. Instead, policy should be focused on prevention of FAS/E and on system-wide methods for coping with it where it does occur. Whatever is written about classroom strategies should be seen as only temporary and less than optimal.

· 6 ·

Support for First Nations to Address Fetal Alcohol Syndrome and Effects

Michael Anthony Hart

While fetal alcohol syndrome and fetal alcohol effects (FAS/E) are a real concern for the general population, they are devastating for First Nations people. Zaleski (1983) presented a study of 173 Saskatchewan children with FAS/E in which 84 percent of the children diagnosed with FAS and 79 percent of the children diagnosed with FAE were of First Nations or Métis origin. In the Yukon, 46 out of 1,000 First Nations people are affected (Asante and Nelms-Matzke 1985). More recently, in their study of one First Nation in Manitoba, Chudley, Moffat, and Kowlessar found that 9.5 percent of the population were diagnosed with FAS/E (Committee on Alcohol and Pregnancy 1997). Chudley and Moffat suggested that this particular community had rates that were 50–60 times higher than the Canadian average (Teichroeb 1997).

Though methodological research factors may distort the true degree of the issue for First Nations communities throughout Canada, it is apparent that FAS/E has greatly impacted First Nations peoples, who form a young population that is growing faster than other segments of Canada's population (Barsh 1994). In light of these factors, service providers working with people affected by FAS/E must be prepared to work with First Nations peoples. Unfortunately, many service providers are ill-prepared to work across cultures (Sue, Ivey and Pedersen 1996).

The Importance of Understanding First Nations Cultures
In a recent documentary titled "David with FAS" (Cardinal and Schreiber 1996), a non–First Nations adoptive parent stated:

> I found it dreadfully painful to watch my sons, both sons, experience such agony as they grew up in trying to be accepted and relating to others, and not being successful, being rejected. Well, both of them also are of Native heritage. And I attributed a lot of that to their Nativity rather than to the fact that they also have fetal alcohol syndrome. We didn't know.

This adoptive parent was finally able to recognize that his sons' experiences were associated with FAS and distinct from their race. However, it took almost eighteen years for him to arrive at this realization. Apparently, the adoptive parent not only lacked awareness of FAS/E but also lacked awareness of First Nations people, culture and experiences. If this parent had had an understanding of FAS/E *and* the culture of his sons, the frustrations faced by this family might not have been as extreme.

Caregivers of people with FAS/E are not the only ones who have exhibited a lack of understanding of First Nations cultures. McCormick (1995: 252) stated that, "after completing my M.A. in counselling psychology, I used traditional Western therapeutic approaches with First Nations people and often found that they were only moderately effective." Broken Nose (1992) noted that not only is it a concern that Western therapeutic approaches may be limited, but there is a realistic risk that service providers may have inaccurate and, at times, racist views of First Nations peoples. Such practice promotes further oppression of First Nations peoples. It is important, then, that service providers demonstrate an understanding of the ethnicity, history and culture of the people served in order to provide good and appropriate services (Broken Nose 1992; Ellison Williams and Williams 1996; Janzen, Skakum and Lightning 1994). At a fundamental level there is a need for knowledge and respect for First Nations world views and value systems in order to create trusting, helping relationships and define the most appropriate intervention (McCormick 1995; Sue, Ivey and Pedersen 1996).

First Nations Cultures and World Views

First Nations people, Métis and Inuit have been defined together by the Constitution Act of 1982 as "aboriginal peoples." However, each of these peoples differ in history, culture and world views. On another level, *First Nations* is an encompassing term used to refer to people such as the Cree, Anishinaabe, Tlingit, Mi'kmaq and Mohawk. While there are many similarities, each of these peoples have their own unique histories, cultures and world views. On a third level, "First Nations" refers to particular communities. Again, there are many similarities between communities, but to speak of these communities as if they were all the same is to neglect their distinctiveness.

On yet another level, Western culture has been imposed, at times violently, upon First Nations people (Barsh 1994; Mawhiney 1995; Tobias 1991). As a result, any particular community or person may have incorporated and may express First Nations and Western cultures to varying degrees (Janzen, Skakum and Lightning 1994; Morrissette, McKenzie and Morrissette 1993). On one end of this continuum are persons and communities who hold world views and practices that are traditional to First

Nations. On the other end are persons and communities who are fully assimilated into Western culture or in a state of complete alienation from both First Nations traditions and Western cultures. Overall, differences must be considered in order to ensure that any service provided to First Nations people is appropriate.

In considering differences, service providers need an understanding of the traditional aspect of First Nations peoples' world views. One of the concepts held in common by many traditional First Nations peoples is the importance of a holistic philosophy (Calliou 1995; Garrett and Myers 1996; McCormick 1995; Regnier 1995). Such a view holds that within every individual each aspect—the physical, emotional, mental and spiritual—is important. The family, community and nation are also important. Together, each of these aspects are part of a larger whole that has been referred to as the circle of life, or the medicine wheel.

Associated with this holistic view are concepts of interconnection, balance and harmony (Garrett and Myers 1996; McCormick 1995; Regnier 1995). Each aspect within and around the individual is connected or has a relationship to all other aspects. One part is not any more important than the others; all are equal but different. Interdependence exists among all parts. When each part is given an equal opportunity to develop, balance is maintained. By respecting and supporting each part and connection in relation to all other parts and connections, harmony can be achieved.

Other key concepts that are significant in the First Nations' world view are change and disharmony. Many of the traditional stories of First Nations peoples contain a central character that can be disruptive and bring about change. Wisahketchahk, Nanaboozoo, Raven and Coyote are a few of these characters. Through these stories, many First Nations people have learned that even though the universe is in balance and harmony, flux, transformation and change still exist (Peat 1994). Indeed, order cannot exist without chaos—both are necessary components of the circle of life. Therefore, each individual, family, community and nation has to determine what they are to learn from disharmony and how they will adjust, because they have no choice but to accept the disruption and challenges that come with it (Garrett and Myers 1996).

These concepts have been addressed here in relation to the human level, but they also apply to the natural world, the universe, human development and social development. In other words, the circle of life represents the total universe and everything in it.

First Nations' Practices to be Considered

In addition to these factors and concepts associated with the traditional First Nations' world view, certain practices have been identified as generally more appropriate than others. Three of these practices are addressed here. The first is the ethic of noninterference (Nelson, Kelley and McPherson 1985). Human relations require close connections, but how these connections are made is also significant. When these connections are based upon the idea of hierarchies and that some people can direct and even coerce other people to follow particular behaviours or think in a particular way, then the practices stemming from these connections interfere with a person, family or community's self-determination. Noninterference means that alternative experiences may be shared, but the final view and action rests with each individual, family, community or nation.

Another practice significant to traditional First Nations is sharing. Sharing was the key to survival for many First Nations. Almost everything was shared, including material articles, food and knowledge. This practice continues today. One of the first events when entering some First Nations homes is the sharing of food. Giveaways and potlatches still occur where goods worth thousands of dollars may be freely given by a person, family or clan. Hoarding or taking more than needed was discouraged in the past and may be looked upon poorly today.

A third practice that is highly significant is respect. Calliou (1995: 67) captured the basis of this respect:

> A premise of the First Nations world is that we unconditionally respect all beings because we all begin as seeds from the same material of this Mother Earth. In the circle, no one individual being (two-legged, four-legged, mineral, plant, etc.) is deemed "more than" or "less than" another, so that treatment which elevates or denigrates one or the other is ruled out. The intent is to honour the similarities of the being in an egalitarian contract based upon dignity, integrity, and respect. Differences are accepted as gifts of diversity from Mother Earth and the Creator.

These concepts and practices mentioned above are significant to traditional First Nations and play a part in the relationship between service providers and First Nations people. Therefore, they should be acknowledged by every service provider and considered and included when working with First Nations people.

Working with First Nations People

Mawhiney (1995) has emphasized that service providers need to acknowledge that their education has likely been based upon a Western world view and, as a result, their awareness of First Nations world views is limited. Therefore, they need to prepare themselves to work with First Nations. One of the most fundamental requirements is learning First Nations history in general and also the histories particular to specific communities

(Janzen, Skakum and Lightning 1994; Mawhiney 1995). Understanding First Nations history from a perspective that respects and includes their views will help service providers see that occurrences such as FAS/E are not based solely upon personal choices made by the biological parents but have deep roots in the barrage of socio-political factors that are intrinsically linked to Western society–First Nations relations. First Nations people have called upon others who provide services to individuals affected by FAS/E to recognize these factors (Erickson 1993; Van Bibber 1992).

When working with First Nations people, service providers need to look honestly at their own attitudes. Janzen, Skakum and Lightning (1994: 90) stated:

> You [the professional service provider] are not coming in there with the attitude of "I'll tell you what to do, I know more than you." Rather, adopt an attitude of acceptance of two unique cultures and what we can do to help one another, from the helping perspective. Let's walk together. We can work something out. Let's work eye to eye, at seeing level, not one on top looking down on the other.

It has been suggested that a service provider should be "a person first and a professional second," and his or her relationships should be ones of mutual sharing, learning and growing (Hampton et al. 1995).

A positive acceptance, particularly of cultural diversity and the uniqueness of First Nations cultures, is needed (Janzen, Skakum and Lightning 1994). More specifically, "it is important to recognize that there are strengths in indigenous identity and traditional practices" (Hampton et al. 1995). Nelson, Kelley and McPherson (1985) have suggested that service providers should establish an environment of support in the here-and-now, as opposed to focusing upon assessments and desired outcomes and dictating direction. Support may be demonstrated by spending time to get to know the people with whom you are working directly and indirectly, exercising patience, especially when communicating, and being willing to include Elders and community healers in the provision of services (Janzen, Skakum and Lightning 1994).

In addressing FAS/E specifically, service providers need to orientate themselves holistically. This may mean that their services should address the physical, emotional, spiritual and mental aspects of the persons with FAS/E. On another level, it may mean that their services should be delivered not only to the individual but also to the family, extended family and community. A holistic orientation should enable service providers to recognize that they are connected to the community, family and individual with FAS/E and that they have to determine how to maintain this connection in a balanced and harmonious manner. Balance and harmony may be achieved by following practices such as those previously noted: respect, sharing and noninterference.

Service providers need to support the view that all people and events are significant in some way to all other people. Garrett and Myers (1996: 96, 99) suggested:

> Everything serves a meaningful and important function in our lives. . . . Because all things are connected like the many strands of a web, and because everything in the Circle of Life affects everything else, we need to develop a greater understanding of our unique place and purpose in the universe. . . . In the traditional way, the idea of seeking resolution of dissonance and discord really encompasses a seeking of harmony and balance among interrelated thoughts, feelings, and actions.

Thus, service providers need to support the discovery of what the person, family and community can learn from FAS/E and how they can still come into balance and harmony with one another despite the challenges FAS/E presents.

On a larger level, services providers need to recognize and respect the self-determination of First Nations communities. These communities are facing numerous concerns and issues, only one of which is FAS/E. While they are acting to try and address all the concerns they possibly can, the resources available to them are limited. They are making many difficult and challenging choices. Recognizing First Nations' self-determination means acknowledging this reality and their rights and responsibilities to control their own destinies.

Finally, service providers need to familiarize themselves with the present repertoire of approaches used to deal with FAS/E. These approaches may be utilized, but first they need to be shared with the First Nations persons, families and communities affected by FAS/E. Such sharing will give them the necessary opportunity to consider each of the approaches and determine the most appropriate ones to be used, if any are to be incorporated at all. In this way, service providers can support the people in their self-determination.

Summary

At one conference where I presented the need to respect, understand and incorporate the First Nations world view into services provided to people with developmental disabilities, a member of the audience responded by saying that these views and practices are nice, but people with developmental disabilities have more important needs; therefore he could not spend his time trying to learn about and provide culturally appropriate services. To say the least, I was disappointed by his response.

Perhaps one of the most important points that service providers must realize and act upon is that culture is central to every person. While issues such as FAS/E deserve significant attention, the importance of this issue or any issue does not pre-empt the fact that culture has to be considered and incorporated when working with First Nations people, especially those facing the issue of FAS/E. People cannot hide behind excuses such as "It is less important" or "We know nothing about First Nations and therefore we cannot do anything about it." If you are going to work to address FAS/E, you can expect to work with First Nations people. If you are going to work with First Nations people, you had better prepare yourself to learn about their cultures and their histories, and how to best support them.

In closing, I would like to share one of many teachings that I have been fortunate enough to receive from an Elder, although a written format is considered a somewhat inappropriate medium for sharing such things. What was shared with me related to the nature of people at the moment of birth. When we are born, we are pure and as close to the Creator as we will ever be during our life on Mother Earth. As babies and small children, we remain close to the Creator. As we grow older and learn how to maintain ourselves on our Mother, we move from this purity and closeness and take on more worldly characteristics. Our spiritual journeys represent our attempts to move back to this purity and closeness to the Creator. For many of us, it takes a lifetime. However, people who face developmental challenges that are attributed to issues such as FAS/E maintain more of their purity and closeness to the Creator than those of us who do not personally face such challenges. As such, those of us without such challenges should treat them with great respect and do our best to support them, even take care of them if need be. In this way, they may help us move closer to the Creator and regain some of our original purity.

The Ecology of FAS/E: Developing an Interdisciplinary Approach to Intervention with Alcohol-affected Children and Their Families

Kathy Jones

B efore the turn of the twentieth century, a small number of medical researchers were speculating on in utero effects for offspring of mothers who consumed alcohol while pregnant (Karp et al. 1995). However, eugenic theory, a transgenerational explanation for "hereditary fee-ble-mindedness," was so thoroughly adopted at that time that all other explanations for developmental childhood concerns were overshadowed. It was not until the early 1970s, when the problem was firmly acknowledged and labelled "fetal alcohol syndrome," that the deleterious impact of in utero exposure to alcohol came to be more widely accepted. A quarter of a century later, we are now beginning to understand the full ecology of fetal alcohol syndrome/fetal alcohol effects (FAS/E). As human service workers in this context, we are seeking to find essential linkages between the community and the affected child within his or her family constellation which will act to provide a comprehensive support network.

Appreciation of diversity is a key starting point for assessment in this field. Diversity is evident in the extreme variations of needs and strengths among individual children. Diversity is also inherent in the living situations of the affected children, a minority of whom live with biological parents or relatives, while most others live with foster families, in group homes and in treatment facilities. From an ecological perspective, community capacities to provide appropriate services and educational and recreational opportunities form another diverse reality. As front-line service providers, we are not only confounded by the range of physical, environmental, emotional and learning needs that children with FAS/E experience, but we are also aware of the compounding issues and problems that permeate the child's home, school and community environments. We have come to recognize that it is not enough to intervene with the child alone.

It is imperative that we understand the full range of environmental factors which come into play regarding an affected child's quality of life and ability to achieve his or her full potential. Societal conditions and pressures often pose significant barriers. While not true of all situations, we have found many instances where the effects of intergenerational poverty, physical and sexual abuse, and systemic racism and sexism are acting to create an environment detrimental to the child's progress. Lacking social supports and a sense of hope for the future, mothers are not discouraged from continuing to use and abuse alcohol and drugs. These social conditions may mean that some affected children have witnessed or been subjected to abuse and neglect early in their lives. In other cases, affected children and their families may have needs which are so severe that early institutionalization or multiple home placements have been a reality. Individual and family needs that are already stressful can be further aggravated if a community misunderstands the physical and emotional needs of alcohol-affected children and their families. A lack of awareness, information and understanding can impose additional hardships when families try to access systems such as schools, social services, health care and recreational programs.

A recognition of the impact of family and community functioning in determining outcomes for children with FAS/E has been well documented by Ann Streissguth (1996) in a study of secondary disabilities. Streissguth notes that environmental influences, including a supportive family and understanding community, play as much a part in good outcomes for FAS/E children as interventions designed specifically for the disability itself. For example, the results of her study indicated that among young adults with FAS/E, over 90 percent have a secondary mental health concern, 60 percent have had some involvement with the legal system and 50 percent have had a history of inappropriate sexual behaviour (1996: 4). Streissguth's research reminds us that in planning for the needs of FAS/E children and their families, it may be as important to intervene with the family and community as it is to provide services directly to the affected child.

Comprehensive Intervention

Because of the diversity of needs and the range of related environmental concerns inherent to this field, an interdisciplinary team using a systemic approach to assessment and intervention holds the best promise for providing good outcomes for alcohol-affected children. Theresa Grant and others, who worked with high-risk addicted mothers, promote a coordinated, comprehensive team strategy for successful intervention with "high need" families (Grant et al. 1996). They note some essential components of a comprehensive intervention model, which include: (1) family-centred intervention reflecting the needs of both the mother and child, (2) a coordinated team approach with opportunities for referral to specialists, (3) emphasis on community-based therapeutic interventions that provide supportive environments for alcohol-affected children and (4) an advocate, case manager or "key person" who is readily accessible to the parent (1996: 1). These components, when transformed into action, suggest several important "points of entry" in developing a systemic model of intervention.

Family-centred Intervention/Advocacy and Case Management

Family-centred intervention must be more than a philosophical stance which respects the role of parents in determining their own family's needs. Each family will bring unique features to the situation, and biological, adoptive and foster families may present needs which require different forms of intervention. Recognizing that needs will shift over time, intervention with a child and family may range from intensive therapeutic involvement with some families to community advocacy on behalf of others.

Practice experience suggests that biological or birth families with alcohol-affected children may be the most needy. Although some (Smith 1992) have argued that addicted parents may have too many of their own issues to be effective parents for alcohol-exposed children, the prevailing trend in child welfare is for children to remain with birth families (Sparks 1993). While some birth families may be thought to unnecessarily expose children to risks of neglect and abuse, some studies show that addicted parents have the cognitive capacity to understand their child's needs and maintain the same parenting expectations for themselves as non-addicted parents (Colton 1982; Davis 1997). However, as a practitioner responsible for the welfare of the child, it is important to recognize that although biological parents may want to raise their children and certainly intend to do their best, they may also have overwhelming emotional and/or physical needs that limit their abilities to effectively parent a high-needs child.

Intervenors with families must also consider the distinct and often severe needs of the child with FAS/E. Unlike other children with physical and mental challenges, many FAS/E children have behavioural disabilities that are exceptionally hard to manage, even for those who are the most experienced. Behaviour disorders often present in the earliest stages of life. Many alcohol-affected babies experience difficulty with feeding, show tactile sensitivity to touch and temperature, and may have extended periods in which they have difficulty sleeping through the night (Kleinfeld and Wescott 1993). In some cases, FAS/E children may have serious medical conditions which demand extended periods of hospitalization and separation from the family. School-aged children who are alcohol-affected often display learning disabilities, speech delays, hyperactivity and aggressive or violent tendencies. They sometimes reject nurturing from others and have significant difficulty developing and maintaining emotional bonds. Parents who are already struggling with their own personal issues need emotional and physical supporters who understand the toll of trying to nurture a baby who is "fussy" or a child who is "difficult." Counselling, respite, community child care programs and real time off can provide parents with the emotional and physical nurturing they may need to continue parenting an alcohol-affected child.

Working with birth families requires careful attention to the type of support provided as well as the values held (overtly or covertly) by the relevant responding systems. For example, birth parents who have a history of alienation from health, educational or social service systems will not likely present to these systems as willing, compliant clients. Traditional service agencies which have grown out of charity or protection movements tend to promote middle-class values. Where these persist, the "client" may feel shame and alienation when he or she cannot achieve the prescribed standards (Kovalesky 1997). It is understandable that parents may have difficulty in admitting that their child could be drug- or alcohol-affected, especially if their fear of disclosure is coupled with a fear that the child may be apprehended by child welfare workers. Kovalesky (1997) notes that, in the United States, up to 55 percent of addicted mothers have lost one or more children to child welfare authorities. Parents who have had past involvement with child welfare systems are often reluctant to disclose any level of difficulty related to the child for fear of being isolated as the source of such troubles. Because many behaviours exhibited by alcohol-affected children look much like behaviour patterns displayed by neglected or abused children, confusion and misunderstanding about "cause" can easily prevail. Sadly, parents who are experiencing "legitimate" problems with their children's behaviour and seriously need external supports may be reluctant to request help. Relationship building with members of the family system, in particular the birth mother, is crucial to successful intervention. All members of the intervention team, including medical personnel, child care workers, specialists, therapists, teachers and child welfare workers, must have sensitive and thorough training to assist them in understanding the delicate balance that may be involved in supporting an affected child who is living with his or her birth family.

Another key area of support in working with birth families relates to advocacy within and between systems. Advocacy, as a responsibility of case management, plays an important part in helping birth parents access services and supports for their FAS/E child. Advocacy roles may include helping parents locate services in the community, attending home and school meetings, mediating between care providers who hold divergent attitudes or just talking with families about everyday problems. The work of Grant et al. (1996: 3) with birth mothers found that a satisfactory relationship between the parent and her advocate was the most critical component in improving outcomes for alcohol-affected children. Further, Grant et al. found that parents who felt listened to and respected often gained the confidence needed to engage in treatment for themselves. Of those participants in the advocacy-based program that they considered, 80 percent had attended an alcohol treatment program (with 43 percent remaining alcohol and drug free), and 57 percent of the parents continued to maintain custody of their children.

While support to birth families may need to begin with building trust between the advocate and the mother, the role of the case manager or advocate who is working with foster and/or adoptive parents may be quite different. Service accessibility may be the key concern for these families. In many cases, the points of intervention may focus on helping parents to access child-specific supports such as child care programs, play therapy, adapted recreational opportunities, classroom aids and occupational or speech therapy. Depending on the degree of service available and the family's circumstances, funding to pay for some of these services may need to be sought. Helping the parents plan and implement a holistic response to the child's needs and successfully recruiting appropriate services can assist the family's efforts to help the child reach his or her maximum potential.

Because several systems might be simultaneously engaged with a child, there often may be professional disagreement over the best strategies, goals and priorities to pursue for a specific child. In such situations, the case manager or advocate may find their primary role expanded to include being a mediator between systems, parents and child, reaching out into the child's school and neighborhood environments. Jan Lutke (1993) notes that foster parents tell her that they often feel the need to be both the service system and the community advocate for their FAS/E child, especially in areas where little information and support exists. Again, the need for educational training and support for foster or adoptive parents is obvious. Several communities now offer support groups for foster parents who are caring for alcohol-affected children in their families. Lutke (1993) and Coles and Platzman (1992) point out that foster-parent support groups provide opportunities for parents to share ideas, resources and strategies. In addition, parents who come together can offer each other the emotional support that prevails when people come to realize that they are not alone in facing the challenges associated with rearing a child with FAS/E.

Children with FAS/E who have experienced separation from their birth families likely bring multiple levels of psycho-social and emotional needs into a foster or adoptive family (Guinta and Streissguth 1988). Family breakdown, abuse traumas and the disruption caused by a series of placements add to relational difficulties for alcohol-affected children. A supportive and clearly predictable environment is essential for affected children to thrive. Because many children with FAS/E experience multiple placements in their primary relational systems, they are at risk for secondary disabilities or concerns. Children denied stability and predictability display attachment and bonding disorders, and face school expulsion. Children with FAS/E are exceptionally vulnerable to peer pressure and tend to experience relatively early involvement in the youth justice system (Streissguth 1996).

Foster parents who have a successful record of caring for a number of children may find themselves stymied when an affected child comes into their home. Even though they have not changed their child care techniques, this particular child appears not to respond to any of the strategies they have successfully employed in the past. Experienced foster parents may find it difficult and embarrassing to bring forward their personal struggles with a child. This occurs most frequently when an alcohol-affected child remains in the child welfare system but is still undiagnosed for FAS/E. Such situations again point out the need for education and training about FAS/E among all members of the child welfare system.

Like birth parents, foster and adoptive parents often feel grief over the discovery of a disability. Frequently they express extreme anger at the birth mother for drinking while pregnant (National Health/Education Consortium 1994). The emotional ramifications of such intense feelings can adversely affect family functioning. A case manager or advocate needs to be prepared to support a foster or adoptive family at these times.

Guinta and Streissguth (1988) argue that the role of the caseworker or professional advocate is a high priority in helping families support alcohol-affected children. However, as suggested by the distinctive needs expressed by birth, foster and adoptive families, the responsive roles expected of the caseworker can be diverse. While birth families might express a need for therapeutic intervention and advocacy for the entire family, adoptive and foster families might well prefer to case-manage their children and use professional support only as a community resource or point of reference. Parents in the second case may profit more from monthly support-group meetings or professional development opportunities than from having an advocate or caseworker visit them weekly or biweekly. However, in both cases, an important role remains for a caseworker/advocate in helping parents access and coordinate the range of therapeutic and community-based supports needed by their children.

Coordinated Teams and Community-based Support

Given the possibility of multiple disabilities, intervention with alcohol-affected children often requires many therapeutic, educational and community-based supports. For example, early intervention specialists who focus primarily on work with preschool children may develop many creative and functional opportunities for these children to meet early developmental goals. Speech and language pathologists may provide support for critical speech enhancement. Occupational therapists intervene to improve fine and gross motor skills; they are also instrumental in assessing a child's physical environment and suggesting ways to reduce problems induced by too much or too little stimulation. Teachers provide adaptive or special education support for children to meet learning goals. As children age, job coaches, community support workers and therapists may be added to the therapeutic team. It is important that a child's needs are regularly assessed as they progress through their lives.

In other human service fields in which caseworkers experience similar challenges, such as work with mental health consumers, school-based programs and services for children with disabilities, the use of interdisciplinary teams has been shown to be an effective way to coordinate a range of needed supports (Abramson 1993; Coles and Platzman 1992). In social service systems, interdisciplinary teams provide opportunities for coordinated interventions that reflect the complexity of services needed for high-risk populations (Billups 1987). In schools, an interdisciplinary focus on developing educational goals allows teachers and therapists to work together with outside agencies to develop a curriculum that meets the special physical, physiological and educational needs of the student (Morgan 1985). Interdisciplinarity also allows opportunities for information and support to move from one system to another, for example, from school to home, thus maintaining consistency for the child.

A team needs to develop a family-centred approach to intervention to be effective in providing therapeutic supports to disabled children. Garshelis and McConnel (1993) argue that parents play an important participatory role in planning for their disabled children. Services that are responsive to the needs of the family lead to greater benefits for both the child and the family (Garshelis and McConnel 1993). Family functioning is strengthened as families begin to incorporate and build on information provided by professional and community supports. Edlefsen and Baird (1994) and Streissguth (1996) suggest that early intervention and specialized services minimize the possibility of secondary or more serious emotional, social and academic problems. However, as Coles and Platzman (1992) point out, traditional forms of family involvement may prove difficult for parents who are addicted and in need of services themselves. Adaptations and adjustments may need to be made to accommodate families with more extensive needs. Guinta and Streissguth (1988) stress that services for high-need families must reflect social and cultural background, class issues and the prior experiences of those accessing service. Respect for diversity is a key element in the assessment process. Accessibility and approachability are essential if the full range of services are to be utilized. Further, goals must respect and reflect the needs of the family, not solely the desires of the professional team. Services that provide noticeable, tangible support to families or offer improvements in functioning for their children will be understood and respected by families over services whose goals for the intended recipients are not concrete.

Finally, it is important to note that social conditions such as poverty, underemployment and unemployment, inadequate housing and limited opportunities for education and training create situations of alienation, powerlessness and hopelessness for many families of alcohol-exposed children. Supports to families must encompass all of these concerns and provide opportunities for women and men to be empowered through treatment, education and employment and to be able to advocate for themselves and their children. Weick (1983) calls this process the "giving over" of power to families, which is an important move towards reaching the goal of self-determination.

Summary
Without a full range of service options for families and children impacted by prenatal exposure to alcohol, the effectiveness of any advocate or case manager is compromised. Unfortunately, most service options are available only in larger urban centres. However, as governments focus on debt reduction at the cost of social, medical and educational services, even the newly emergent programs that are beginning to address the myriad of needs in the FAS/E field are jeopardized. Funding cuts to early intervention programs, schools and community agencies will seriously compromise the range of services available to affected children, their families and communities, thus potentially creating a critical situation and impossible dilemma for many families who are attempting to raise alcohol-affected children. The community must be determined to take a stand by providing real supports to women and their families before we will see an elimination of the effects of alcohol and drug use on tomorrow's children.

· 8 ·

Poverty, Policies of Disentitlement and FAS/E

Gordon Ternowetsky

The often tragic and difficult outcomes of fetal alcohol syndrome/fetal alcohol effects (FAS/E) on children, their families and caregivers are increasingly clear. So too are the issues facing human service workers who have the responsibility for providing help to those who turn to them for assistance in dealing with FAS/E. However, our understanding of FAS/E is still in its infancy and there remains a large gap between its diagnosis and workable interventions. Considerable work is still required to develop appropriate secondary and tertiary interventions for FAS/E.

The most effective way of dealing with FAS/E is to prevent its occurrence. We know from the etiology of FAS/E that its roots lie to a large extent in poverty and the economic and social marginalization that poverty produces. These circumstances not only restrict people's opportunities and life chances but can lead to the maladaptive behaviours and lifestyles to which FAS/E is often attributed. The best form of prevention lies, therefore, in fashioning policies that will eliminate the structural factors that create and maintain poverty. Recent progress on this front is, however, discouraging. In the last decade and a half, we have lost ground in our efforts to curtail poverty in Canadian society. Poverty is on the rise and, as it affects more people, its outcomes—such as poor physical and emotional health, inadequate nutrition, low-standard housing, higher infant mortality rates, substance abuse and FAS/E will continue to increase. This chapter considers why this is happening. It looks first at salient changes in the structure of our economy that have led to a decline in economic security and the growing impoverishment of an increasing number of individuals, families and children. It then considers the changing role of the state in dealing with poverty and its effects on people.

A number of factors are responsible for the rise in poverty and the growing economic uncertainties of Canadians. These include the persistence of historically high levels of unemployment in both good and bad economic times; the restructuring of labour markets that have led to an expansion of low-paid jobs and a decline in better-paid employment; the growing labour-force participation of women, who continue to occupy the most insecure, often part-time, low-waged work; the stagnation of incomes; the substantial downsizing in good-paying public sector employment; and the increased globalization of production which offers a justification for companies to keep wages low, eliminate staff and shut down plants in order to remain competitive (Pulkingham and Ternowetsky 1997).

Despite the strong levels of economic growth currently witnessed in Canada, the restructuring of labour markets has resulted in increased economic marginality and growing levels of family and child poverty. The impact of these labour market changes on poverty are well documented. Data from 1984 to 1994 (NCW 1996) depicts a clear relationship between the growth of unemployment, poverty and welfare dependency. As the unemployment rate rises, so does poverty and the number of people dependent on income assistance. A "good job" according to the Council, "is the best assurance against poverty" (NCW 1996). The Canadian Centre for Policy Alternatives (1997: 26) also shows that "[w]hen the unemployment rate drops by one percentage point, the child poverty rate falls accordingly by the same extent, or about 70,000 children."

Perhaps the clearest impact of the restructuring of labour markets on poverty is presented by Campaign 2000, a national coalition of organizations which monitors changes in child and family poverty in Canada. In its 1997 *Report Card*, this coalition reported that the "number of poor children [grew] from 934,000 in 1989 to 1,472,000 in 1995—an increase of 58%" (Campaign 2000 1997: 3). Poor children, however, come from poor families and the impact of the availability and quality of jobs on family and child poverty is clear in its report. Between 1989 and 1995, children in poor families where "at least one parent is unemployed for more than 6 months increased from 570,000 . . . to 835,000"—a growth of 47 percent. Regarding the changing nature and remuneration of jobs, the number of children raised in poor families where a parent is working full-time climbed to 433,000 in 1995, an increase of almost 30 percent from 1989; this rises to 43 percent when children in families with parents working both full- and part-time are considered. In today's "new economy" of low-paying, nonstandard and insecure employment, many parents working full-time "can't earn enough money" to lift themselves out of poverty (Campaign 2000 1997: 7). Estimates by the National Council of Welfare (1995) indicate that close to a quarter of poor families have a head who works full-time, a figure that suggests families are being pulled into poverty by the spread of low-wage jobs.

How are governments responding to the growth of poverty in Canada? And what does the future seem to hold for the development of social policies designed to alleviate poverty? To answer these questions we need to consider the impact of neo-liberalism, the economic philosophy that has reshaped the making of social policy in Canada since the mid-1980s.

Neo-liberalism asserts the primacy of the market and the need to limit the scope of state intervention. According to this framework, a welfare state prevents markets from working efficiently. It creates market disincentives through the excessive tax burdens required to fund a welfare state, and through programs such as unemployment insurance and welfare assistance that permit people to choose leisure over work. During the 1980s under the Mulroney Conservatives, and now in the 1990s under the Chrétien Liberals, these neo-liberal prescriptions have been implemented through a range of policies that focus on deficit and debt control, spending restraint, less government and a restructuring of the Canadian welfare state that has resulted in a withdrawal of state protection in the midst of increased labour market insecurity, poverty and economic uncertainty (Pulkingham and Ternowetsky 1996 and 1997).

The post-1996 years represent a decisive turning point for Canadian social policy. For example, the introduction of Bill C-21, the new Employment Insurance (EI) legislation, sharply curtails entitlements and benefit levels for jobless people. Several studies (CCSD 1996a; Pulkingham 1997) point out that it is now more difficult for people to qualify for benefits if they work between fifteen and thirty-four hours per week or hold temporary employment. Changes in the calculation of benefits also means that close to 15 percent of claimants will see benefit reductions of approximately 25 percent. The lowered maximum insurable earnings level of $39,000 (down from $42,380) will also, according to the Canadian Council of Social Development (1996a: 3), "reduce the security of millions of workers." EI also introduces penalties for repeat users that, together with the "high income clawback," will lower benefits for some million claimants and penalize workers for taking seasonal and temporary employment. In today's economy, where nonstandard jobs are increasing, this new legislation ends up disentitling people, exacerbating the economic insecurities that accompany job loss and reducing the levels of income protection needed to keep people from falling into poverty. Indeed, in November 1996 the number of unemployed workers entitled to jobless benefits dropped to under 40 percent, down from levels of entitlement that exceeded 90 percent in the late 1970s (CCPA 1997; Statistics Canada 1997).

The most important legislation limiting the scope, generosity and the Canadian welfare state's ability to curtail poverty and its consequences is the Canada Health and Social Transfer (CHST), introduced in April 1996. Prior to this measure, welfare provisions designed to protect the living standards of the poor and most vulnerable were financed through the cost-shared, federal-provincial funding agreements of the Canada Assistance Plan (CAP). The implications of the CHST for antipoverty strategies are considerable. First, lower federal transfers to the provinces were introduced along with the CHST. At the same time, legally mandated CAP services meant to "help lessen, remove or prevent the causes and effect of poverty, child neglect and dependence on public assistance" (Canada 1985: 1) have been cast aside with the introduction of the CHST. Without the obligation to provide supports previously mandated by CAP, it is likely that "services for child protection . . . family counselling, rape crisis centres, shelters for women and subsidized day care" will be watered down or disappear in a number of provinces and territories (CCSD 1996c: 2; Torjman 1995: 1).

Second, the CHST is a block fund that provides federal money for provincially administered health, education and welfare programs. In its first two years (1996/97 to 1998/99) the CHST means a loss of some $7 billion for the provinces. There is now less money available to the provinces to deal with increased safety-net demands. This reduced funding means that provincial income assistance rates likely will deteriorate, further entrenching the poverty of those dependent on welfare. Another point is that the CHST does not stipulate how this transfer is to be spent (i.e., for health, education or welfare, or any of these areas), and monies traditionally earmarked for welfare can now be channeled by the provinces to other areas.

Third, under CAP the provinces had to comply with federally established national standards in order to receive funding for their welfare programs. Most of these conditions are gone with the CHST. No longer are provinces obliged to provide assistance to people judged in need; the requirement to ensure that provincial income-assistance benefits are tied to the cost of basic needs has also disappeared; a ban on imposing a work test as a condition for receipt of benefits is gone, as is the requirement for provinces to establish an appeals mechanism for individuals to challenge welfare decisions. The elimination of these standards, particularly the principle of entitlement, opens the way for provinces and territories to deny assistance to those in need (CCSD 1996b). This is now occurring as people are being denied assistance in a number of jurisdictions, even though they have a demonstrated need and, in some cases, no financial resources whatsoever (NAPO 1997; NCW 1997; Edmonton Social Planning Council 1997).

Finally, the CHST means "a reduced federal presence in human services—and a diminished ability to ensure and enforce any meaningful national standards" (Torjman and Battle 1995: 1). Provinces now have few restrictions in developing their own forms of the safety net. This has led to more residual and minimalist programs of last resort with a fragmented patchwork of increasingly different provincial welfare programs. The CHST, which accelerates the downloading of federal responsibilities to the provinces and municipalities, is the legislative framework that has made this possible. This is the context in which future antipoverty policies will be fashioned in different jurisdictions across the nation. What can we expect?

Some answers to this question are already clear. The National Anti-Poverty Organization's (1997) review of provincial/territorial welfare programs finds a growing patchwork of diverse programs that are characterized by increasingly punitive, restrictive and minimalist welfare provisions. This research shows that provincial income assistance rates are falling and are not adjusted to the cost of living; funding for basic needs in emergency situations is being curtailed and/or denied; work or training for social assistance is becoming mandatory in many jurisdictions; increased eligibility requirements are making it difficult for individuals in need to apply for welfare, and people are being disqualified upon application even when they have no income. The impact of this erosion of formal income provisions puts added pressure on the informal sector of support provided by friends, families, communities and the third sector. Research in Ontario (SPCMT 1996) also reports that alongside cuts in welfare rates and stricter eligibility criteria, there are also substantial cuts to nonprofit community organizations. This Ontario study depicts a disappearing social service sector and concludes that, increasingly, the responsibility for those in need will fall on the informal support sector and charitable organizations such as food banks.

In a review of the implications of the CHST for the delivery of social programs, Bach and Rioux (1996) predicted that the offloading of responsibilities to provinces and municipalities, in the context of reduced funding and high demand, will lead to greater targeting of benefits according to the "worthiness" or "unworthiness" of those seeking help. This is now taking place. Many provinces (as well as the federal government) are dividing the poor into two categories: the "deserving poor" (the working poor, children and the disabled) and the "undeserving poor" (adults deemed employable, including parents with increasingly younger children who are in receipt of welfare benefits). The imposition of mandatory "workfare" as a condition for the receipt of benefits is one example of a policy based on this distinction. Workfare programs are build around an assumption that the cause of dependency stems from "moral character or values" rather than structural issues that lead to high employment and dependency (Struthers 1996). Another example is the Family Bonus component of B.C. Benefits in British Columbia, a $103 a month benefit for each child in low to modest income families with a parent in the paid workforce. Poor families whose income comes from welfare are not eligible for this benefit. Targeting benefits according to the work status of parents is also a central component of the new National Child Benefit recently introduced by Ottawa and the provinces. Here we have an enriched benefit that is earmarked for poor children but is only available to families whose main source of income comes from employment. In practice this means that more than 60 percent of Canada's poor children will gain nothing financially from this new program (Valpy 1997). This policy of excluding welfare families with children (the "undeserving poor") and targeting benefits to families with a parent in the workforce (the "deserving poor") results in the denial of additional assistance to the poorest of poor families and children. The outcome of this policy of disentitlement is to further increase the economic vulnerability of those in greatest need.

This chapter has touched briefly on the unfolding context of poverty and the way it is being managed in Canadian society. On one front, the opportunity structure for many in Canadian society is collapsing. High levels of unemployment and the spread of poor-paying jobs are keeping people poor. For many, even the wages of full-time, full-year work are too low to permit an escape from poverty. On another front, the remaking of social policies in recent years has resulted in a more selective, residual and punitive form of state protection for the poor. Income assistance benefits are declining, support services are increasingly uncertain and those in need are being screened out, disentitled and forced to turn to friends, families and charities for survival. Canada's safety net is unravelling. Our future prospects of effectively addressing the correlates of poverty such as low standard housing, poor health, unsafe lifestyles and FAS/E will remain bleak unless we establish a new, collective commitment to significantly reduce the level of poverty in this country.

Case Management with FAS/E Children in Northern and Remote Communities

Jeanette Turpin and Glen Schmidt

In the past thirty years, an extensive body of literature has documented the deleterious effects of alcohol consumption during pregnancy (Lemoine et al. 1968; Jones et al. 1973; Majewski and Goecke 1982). Children born to women who have ingested alcohol during pregnancy can exhibit a multitude of lifelong problems with considerable variability in their levels of physical, behavioural, psychological and cognitive deficits. Fetal alcohol syndrome (FAS) and the more subtle fetal alcohol effects (FAE) are medical terms used to describe such individuals.

Although there is individual variation, the debilitating effects of FAS and FAE are similar. The area of greatest concern is the damage caused to the central nervous system. Two of the most compromised areas in this region are the neuropsychological (most notably intelligence) and behaviour/learning functions. The resulting difficulties create great challenges for both the developing child and his or her caregivers.

Family Situations of Children with FAS/E

The quality of the home environment does not ameliorate the damage caused by prenatal exposure to alcohol. However, achievement of an optimal outcome requires the family situation to be structured, predictable and routine. FAS/E children with their multitude of problems can test all of the abilities of parents and caregivers. Burnout is a common problem encountered by even the most functional of families. Although a stable family environment is not a panacea for FAS/E, it is clearly required to maximize an affected child's potential.

The long-term research done on FAS/E shows alarming patterns in the family situations of these children. As a group, mothers who give birth to children with FAS are usually chronic alcoholics or individuals who severely abuse alcohol during their pregnancy (Majewski and Goecke 1982; Streissguth and Guinta 1988). Fathers are also likely to have drug and alcohol problems and they frequently abandon their parental responsibility. Studies concerning children born to heavy-drinking mothers describe their family environments as "remarkably unstable" (King 1991). King refers to one long-term study by Streissguth, Clarren and Jones (1985) of sixty-one adolescents and adults (average age seventeen) which states that, on average, individuals "lived in five different homes . . . only nine percent were still with both biological parents and only three percent still with their biological mothers. Nearly one-third were never cared for by their biological mothers, they were abandoned in the hospital or given up for adoption. Of the children for whom accurate data could be obtained, 69 percent of the biological mothers were dead. Many died from alcohol-related illnesses, suicide, homicide, falls and auto accidents" (King 1991). In another study by Dr. Streissguth and her colleagues, similar findings were noted. Of the fifty-two FAS and FAE patients studied, "31 percent of the patients had never been cared for by their biological mother, 77 percent did not live with either biological parent, 26 percent were in foster homes, 21 percent were with relatives, 16 percent had been adopted and 9 percent were in group homes or institutions" (Streissguth, Aase, Clarren et al. 1991).

It is not just chronic alcoholism that results in children being born with FAS/E. For example, the social drinker who subsequently gives birth to an FAS/E child may not have realized she was pregnant until it was too late. Most social-drinking mothers generally cease their alcohol intake once they become aware of their pregnancy. Even with the increasing awareness regarding alcohol's damage to the fetus, there are some parents and health professionals who continue to believe that one or two drinks every now and then during pregnancy won't hurt.

Regardless of the diagnosis, the research widely acknowledges the poor prognosis for many children raised in a milieu of alcohol abuse. In these environments, family situations are generally unstable and poverty is often a compounding factor. However, common understanding of substance abuse shifts the focus toward the addiction of the parent rather than the needs of the child. This has proven detrimental for most children and only serves to exacerbate the problems associated with FAS/E. In these situations the degree of risk posed to the child is usually underestimated.

Risk assessment tools generally pay heed to the fact that children with FAS/E are at increased risk for child abuse. However, the same tools assume knowledge of, or intent to obtain, a diagnosis. This is often a mistaken assumption, as demonstrated by Turpin (1996). Turpin's study of a group of child protection workers in British Columbia revealed that less than 10 percent were able to correctly state the main characteristics in the diagnosis of FAS/E. While these results cannot be generalized, it is probable that risk assessment tools which assume knowledge of FAS/E will miss identifying many of the children who are potentially at important risk. Lack of access to specialist resources is likely to result in further difficulty in obtaining accurate assessments of risk. In more remote parts of the country this problem presents a major challenge.

Resource Issues for FAS/E Individuals in Northern and Remote Areas

Resources to support children with FAS/E are generally in short supply, if available at all. This problem is much more acute in northern and remote regions of Canada. Northerners have always felt shortchanged compared to their urban counterparts when it comes to accessing the comprehensive services required to deal with a challenging condition such as FAS/E. Furthermore, the urban-designed policies and programs which are available often prove to be ineffective or difficult to implement in less densely populated areas. The geographical expanse of the North makes it financially impractical to fund comprehensive services to all northern locations. Consequently, major centres such as Prince George in British Columbia, Whitehorse in the Yukon, and Iqaluit in the Northwest Territories provide northern and remote locations with regional access to the more specialized services. Cutbacks in health care, social services and education are currently taking place under the guise of reducing the government deficit and this further aggravates northerners, who already feel like the poor cousin. Although northerners have put up with this arrangement in the past, they are now becoming more vocal in their disapproval.

For FAS/E children, whose problems require access to a multitude of resources, development of comprehensive services is important. Inability to recruit and retain specialized medical professionals in the North has always been an issue. Primary care professionals (doctors, mental health workers) and educators in many of the rural areas generally do not have the knowledge to diagnose and/or treat FAS/E. Most of the health care professionals who serve local areas are not specialists and are often new to their respective fields. Consequently they do not have the experience, expertise or colleagues immediately available for collaboration or consultation on issues such as FAS/E (Given, Given and Harlan 1994; British Columbia 1995). If the major centres are fortunate enough to have trained staff, the lack of access to public transportation and the cost of travelling to these areas, especially for ongoing treatment or follow-up, can be prohibitive for most families (Zapf 1985).

These various concerns become more pronounced when we talk about the awareness and skill that is required to work with FAS/E children. The reason most often cited for the lack of qualified staff in dealing with this issue relates to the low wage that is paid, especially to paraprofessionals, for these services. Consequently, an agency's ability to attract staff with the necessary skills who are willing to relocate to remote communities becomes compromised. This in turn impacts on the development of effective case management services for FAS/E children. Without sound case management strategies, the situation for children with FAS/E can become even more desperate. In northern and remote areas the more traditional forms of case management are not necessarily the best response.

Case Management

Rothman (1991) has stated that the meaning attached to the concept of *case management* is vague and often unclear. While it is obvious that definitions vary, there is general agreement that case management involves the planned coordination and delivery of services to defined individuals or groups. Betsy Vourlekis (in Vourlekis and Greene 1992) has stated that social workers have been doing just that for years but have called it "case work." Today, however, case management is frequently presented as something new and different. This has occurred for several reasons. Changes in the delivery methods of mental health and health care have been especially important in the growing popularity of the concept. The shift from institution-based care to community-based care has been a powerful force in driving the development of contemporary case-management methods and approaches (Polanka 1969; Willard 1970).

A second reason for renewed interest in case management relates to structural change in the delivery of social work services. Schilling, Schinke and Weatherly (1988) argue that the reality of shrinking resources makes it more difficult for social workers and others to provide direct services and continuously obligates them to develop new tactics to squeeze services from a shrinking resource pool. This is a valid critique, but it can lead to a pejorative view of the concept of case management. Conclusions may develop which see case management itself as the problem, resulting in unwarranted attacks on the concept when the real problem lies in the political decisions that drive the system.

A third factor contributing to renewed interest in case management has to do with the growing complexity of service delivery. New problems and challenges are continually defined and services become highly specialized. Halfon, Berkowitz and Klee (1993) note that children with increasingly complex problems rooted in poverty, child abuse, drug exposure (FAS/E children), family violence and psychiatric disorders defy simple solutions and require coordination of interventions at both a structural and individual level. The knowledge explosion makes it more difficult for the social worker to be "expert" in all these areas. This reality creates the need to use a variety of people and resources in effective forms of service delivery that include skilled coordination and management. As a result, good case-management skills are seen as an integral part of professional social work in contemporary society.

Models of Case Management

Models of case management are perhaps too numerous to count. In Carter's (1995) survey of the literature, she states that there may be up to three hundred different models of case management. Some of these models are defined on the basis of how the actual service is delivered, such as the "brokerage model" or the "interdisciplinary model." Models are also defined according to the frequency of contact between the case manager and the client, an example being the "intensive case management model." Still other models are constructed on a philosophical or value base of serving a particular population. Anthony's model of psychosocial rehabilitation is a value-driven model that sees the case manager form a collaborative partnership with the consumer designed to maximize choice and achieve optimum mental health regardless of disability (Anthony, Cohen and Farkas 1990). A great deal of the diversity in case management models occurs because of variations in configuration. For example, the so-called "strengths," or "independence from welfare," model (Rapp and Chamberlain 1985; Huxley 1993) may take various forms, depending upon who occupies the role of case manager. The case manager could be the social worker, the client or a family member. The distinguishing characteristic of focusing on the client's strengths instead of their deficiencies remains, but the change in manager creates permutations and variations in the model.

Carter (1995) has suggested that it is useful to examine case management models on a child-welfare continuum. On one end are the strengths model and the interdisciplinary model, both emphasizing the importance of high levels of case manager involvement and accountability. Situated at the opposite end are the "broker model" and the "family group conference model," which focus on the importance of the client and family in developing and implementing the service plan. The role of the case manager is secondary and relates to simple coordination and administration processes. The ends of the continuum are likely to differ in terms of the amount of direct worker intervention within the immediate client system, the degree to which the worker is prepared to exercise power and the amount of accountability carried by the social worker.

Huxley (1993) has suggested that while case management models are numerous, there is general agreement on the "core pattern of case management functions." These functions are: assessment, care planning, direct and indirect intervention, monitoring, review and evaluation. The report of the Gove Inquiry into Child Protection (Gove 1995) suggests that responsible attention to these particular functions may be more critical than the model itself. It is also clear that the type of case management model employed must fit the unique characteristics of the population being served. In child welfare services, this must begin with an acknowledgement of the vulnerability of children and the fact that children often lack a voice. Case management in child welfare is not just supportive; it also comes as part of a statutory mandate to protect the health and safety of children. At the very least, case managers must be accountable for the health and safety of the child.

A Northern Model of Case Management for FAS/E Children

There are some major challenges to be overcome in developing a case management model for families and caregivers of FAS/E children who reside in remote northern communities. Levels of alcohol consumption in the North are high and the limited prevalence data seems to suggest that the incidence of FAS/E is also higher in the North (Asante 1981; Robinson, Conry and Conry 1987). This creates a demand for service in an environment where there is a scarcity of resources for the child. One also needs to remember that it is not only the child who requires resources and support. Ultimately it is the caregivers who are left with the need to provide care and guidance to the FAS/E child.

The characteristics of FAS/E children suggest that they are likely to be highly demanding of caregivers and consequently caregivers will require considerable support. The demanding nature of FAS/E, combined with a shortage of knowledgeable caregivers, suggests that a "pedagogically-intensive case management model" is warranted, with the social worker acting as case manager. As in any intensive model of case management, contact with the client is frequent and aggressively initiated by the case manager. The model implicitly includes the basic case management functions as described by Huxley (1993): assessment, care planning, direct and indirect intervention, monitoring, review and evaluation. However, this model has a number of unique requirements related to the case manager's knowledge of FAS/E, the case manager's pedagogic, group leadership, and human resource recruitment skills, and caseload size.

1. *The case manager's knowledge of FAS/E.* Unlike urban centres which have an abundance of specialists, remote northern communities have few "experts." As a result, the social worker/case manager must have a thorough knowledge base related to understanding the behaviour of FAS/E, life-cycle developments for FAS/E-affected persons, and appropriate treatment and management strategies in the home and in the community. Specific information of this kind is generally not part of an undergraduate social work curriculum. Consequently, post-degree, specialized training is required for social workers who will be fulfilling this type of case management role in northern and remote communities.

2. *The case manager's pedagogic skills.* In assembling the range of resources required to support optimum development of the FAS/E child, the social worker/case manager must have the skills and ability to instruct

other caregivers regarding management of the FAS/E child. This necessitates an understanding and ability to operationalize principles of adult learning, as well as the ability to search available literature and assemble current information for the relevant caregivers. Social workers are not necessarily trained to be educators, but skills in the areas of identifying personal strengths and abilities, support, group dynamics, goal setting and motivation fit well with principles of pedagogy. Additional training is required in order to become proficient at developing and delivering curriculum within an adult learning paradigm.

3. *The case manager's group leadership skills.* The case management process for FAS/E individuals in small remote communities will assume an interdisciplinary approach whenever possible. The social worker/case manager must be able to mobilize the skills and abilities of a varied group that may include parents or foster parents, child care workers, homemakers, teachers and physicians. Good communication, thorough planning, regular reviews and clear, agreed-upon evaluative mechanisms are all critical in an interdisciplinary approach. Current undergraduate curriculums do not routinely prepare social workers for the interdisciplinary work that is a reality of contemporary practice. The difficult access to specialists requires a strategy that maximizes the existing pool of human resources. This can only occur if people are prepared to work in a coordinated, interdisciplinary manner.

4. *Human resource recruitment.* In northern and remote communities, the "front line" caregivers will most often be untrained and inexperienced. Historically, single-industry towns located in remote, isolated areas have experienced high levels of population transiency. A stable, experienced resource pool of paraprofessionals is difficult to maintain. As a result, social worker/case managers must have skills in human resource recruitment and support.

5. *Caseload size.* The nature of intensive case management requires the social worker/case manager to have frequent and regular contact with the client and the caregivers. The social worker/case manager must have the flexibility to respond to crisis situations as well as provide ongoing support to people who will frequently be frustrated and exhausted by the demands of care provision. As a consequence, caseload size must be small, numbering no more than ten. The reality of course is that caseloads are high and the case management approach in many jurisdictions has been that of a brokerage model. This loose method of case management allows workers to carry higher caseloads, but contact with clients and contracted care providers is limited. In order to operate a pedagogically-intensive model of case management, additional social work resources are required or there has to be a restructuring of existing agency resources to free up the necessary worker time to operate this model.

Summary

It is clear that there are no easy answers to providing care for the child affected by FAS/E. However, a favourable outcome can only be attained through an intensive case management process that incorporates elements of pedagogy and an effective interdisciplinary approach. This is especially important for northern and remote communities where skilled human resources are in short supply. Failure to adjust the nature and pattern of service delivery will mean that the needs of children with FAS/E continue to be met in a marginal and inadequate manner.

References

Abramson, J. 1993. "Orienting Social Work Employees in Interdisciplinary Settings: Shaping Professional and Organizational Perspectives." *Social Work* 38(2): 152–57.

Alexander-Roberts, C. 1994. *The ADHD Parenting Book*. Dallas: Taylor.

American Educational Research Association, American Psychological Association and National Council on Measurement in Education. 1985. *Standards for Educational and Psychological Testing*. Washington, D.C.: American Psychological Association.

American Psychiatric Association. 1994. *Diagnostic and Statistical Manual of Mental Disorders*. Fourth edition. Washington, D.C.: American Psychiatric Association.

Anastasi, A. 1988. *Psychological Testing*. Sixth edition. New York: MacMillan.

Anthony, W., M. Cohen and M. Farkas. 1990. *Psychiatric Rehabilitation*. Boston: Boston University Center for Psychiatric Rehabilitation.

Asante, K.O. 1981. "FAS in Northwest B.C. and the Yukon." *British Columbia Medical Journal* 23(7): 332–35.

—————, and J. Nelms-Matzke. 1985. *The Survey of Children with Chronic Handicaps and Fetal Alcohol Syndrome in the Yukon and Northwest British Columbia*. Presented to the Council for Yukon Indians. Whitehorse, Yukon.

Bach, M., and M. Rioux. 1996. "Social Policy, Devolution and Disability: Back to Notions of the Worthy Poor." In J. Pulkingham and G. Ternowetsky (eds.), *Remaking Canadian Social Policy: Social Security in the Late 1990s*. Halifax: Fernwood.

Barsh, R.L. 1994. "Canada's Aboriginal Peoples: Social Integration or Disintegration?" *Canadian Journal of Native Studies* 14(1): 1–46.

Becker, M., G. Warr-Leeper and H. Leeper. 1990. "Fetal Alcohol Syndrome: A Description of Oral, Motor, Articulatory, Short-Term Memory, Grammatical and Semantic Abilities." *Journal of Communication Disorders* 23: 97–124.

Billups, J. 1987. "Interprofessional Team Process." *Theory into Practice* 26(2): 146–52.

Blanchard, E.L. 1983. "The Growth and Development of American Indian and Alaskan Native Children." In G.J. Powell (ed.), *The Psychosocial Development of Minority Group Children*. New York: Brunner/Mazel.

Bloom, B.S. 1964. *Stability and Change in Human Characteristics*. New York: Wiley.

Breland, H.M. 1979. *Population Validity and College Entrance Measures*. New York: College Board.

British Columbia. 1996. *Teaching Students with Fetal Alcohol Syndrome/Effects: A Resource Guide for Teachers*. Victoria, B.C.: Ministry of Education, Special Programs Branch.

—————. 1995. *Report of the Northern and Rural Health Task Force*. Victoria, B.C.: Ministry of Health and Ministry Responsible for Seniors.

Brody, N. 1992. *Intelligence*. Second edition. New York: Academic Press.

Broken Nose, M.A. 1992. "Working with the Oglala Lakota: An Outsider's

References

Perspective." *Families in Society: The Journal of Contemporary Human Services* 73(6): 380–84.

Bulhan, H.A. 1985. "Black Americans and Psychopathology: An Overview of Research and Theory." *Psychotherapy* 22: 370–78.

Burd, L., and M. Moffat. 1994. "Fetal Alcohol Syndrome in American Indians, Alaska Natives, and Canadian Aboriginal Peoples: A Review of the Literature. *Public Health Reports* 109(5): 688–93.

Burgess, D., and A. Streissguth. 1992. "Fetal Alcohol Syndrome and Fetal Alcohol Effects: Principles for Educators." *Phi Delta Kappan* 74(1): 24–30.

Burke, S., A. Sayers, A. Baumgart and J. Wray. 1985. "Pitfalls in Cross-Cultural Use of the Denver Developmental Screening Test: Cree Indian Children." *Canadian Journal of Public Health* 76: 303–7.

Calliou, S. 1995. "Peacekeeping Actions at Home: A Medicine Wheel Model for a Peacekeeping Pedagogy." In M. Battiste and J. Barman (eds.), *First Nations Education in Canada: The Circle Unfolds*. Vancouver: UBC Press.

Campaign 2000. 1997. *Child Poverty in Canada: Report Card 1997*. Toronto: Campaign 2000.

Canada. 1985. *Notes on Welfare Services under the Canada Assistance Plan*. Ottawa: Minister of National Health and Welfare.

——————. 1992. Standing Committee on Health and Welfare, Social Affairs, Seniors and the Status of Women. *Foetal Alcohol Syndrome: A Preventable Tragedy*. Ottawa: Government of Canada; Queen's Printer.

Canadian Centre for Policy Alternatives (CCPA). 1997. *The Alternative Federal Budget Framework Document*. Ottawa: CCPA.

Canadian Council on Social Development (CCSD). 1996a. *CCSD Response to Bill C-12: An Act Respecting Employment Insurance in Canada*. Ottawa: CCSD.

——————. 1996b. "Maintaining a National Social Safety Net: Recommendations on the Canada Health and Social Transfer." Position statement. Ottawa: CCSD.

——————. 1996c. *Social Policy Beyond the Budget*. Ottawa: CCSD.

Cardinal, G. (director, producer), and D. Schreiber (producer). 1996. *David with FAS*. Video Kanata Productions in Cooperation with the National Film Board of Canada, Northwest Centre and CBC Newsworld.

Carter, B. 1995. *Case Management Review and Analysis of Child Protection Services in the Province of British Columbia, 1986–1994*. An unpublished background research paper prepared for the Gove Inquiry into Child Protection.

Cazden, C. 1988. *Classroom Discourse*. Portsmouth, N.H.: Heinemann.

Church, M.W., and J. Kaltenbach. 1997. "Hearing, Speech, Language, and Vestibular Disorders in the Fetal Alcohol Syndrome: A Literature Review." *Alcoholism: Clinical and Experimental Research* 21: 495–512.

Clarren, S.K., D. Bowden and S. Astley. 1985. "The Brain in the Fetal Alcohol Syndrome." *Alcohol Health and Research World* 10(1): 20–23.

Coles, C., and K. Platzman. 1992. "Fetal Alcohol Effects in Preschool Children: Research, Prevention and Intervention." In *Identifying the Needs of Drug-Affected Children: Public Policy Issues* (OSAP monograph no. 11). Maryland: U.S. Department of Health and Human Services.

Colton, M. 1982. "Attitudes, Experiences, and Self-Perception of Heroin Addicted

Mothers." *Journal of Social Issues* 38: 78–92.

Committee on Alcohol and Pregnancy. 1997. "A Prevalence of Fetal Alcohol Syndrome and Fetal Alcohol Effects in One American Indian Community in Canada." *Manitoba F.A.S. News* 3(1): 3.

Connor, P., and A. Streissguth. 1996. "Effects of Prenatal Alcohol Exposure Across the Life Span." *Alcohol Health and Research World* 20: 170–74.

Cuellar, I., and R. Roberts. 1984. "Psychological Disorders Among Chicanos." In J.L. Martinez and R.H. Mendoza (eds.), *Chicano Psychology*. New York: Academic Press.

Dasen, P.R. 1977. *Piagetian Psychology: Cross-Cultural Contributions*. New York: Gardner Press.

Davis, D. 1994. *Reaching Out to Children with FAS/FAE*. New York: Simon & Schuster.

Davis, S. 1997. "Comprehensive Interventions for Alcohol Affecting the Parenting Effectiveness of Chemically Dependent Women." *Journal of Obstetric, Gynecologic and Neonatal Nursing* 26(5): 604–10.

de la Cruz, E., and L. Brandt. 1995. "When is Writers' Workshop Writers' Workshop?" *Journal of Classroom Interaction* 30(1): 21–28.

Demchak, M., and S. Drinkwater. 1993. "Best Practices in Assessing Adaptive Behaviour." In H.B. Vance (ed.), *Best Practices in Assessment for School and Clinical Settings*. Brandon, Vt.: Clinical Psychology Publishing.

Dorris, M. 1989. *The Broken Cord*. New York: Harper and Row.

Edelstein, S. 1995. *Children with Prenatal Alcohol and/or Drug Exposure: Weighing the Risks of Adoption*. Washington, D.C.: CWLA Press.

Edlefsen, M., and M. Baird. 1994. "Making it Work: Preventive Mental Health Care for Disadvantaged Preschoolers." *Social Work* 39(5): 566–73.

Edmonton Social Planning Council. 1997. *Poverty Trends in Edmonton: The Race to the Bottom Heats Up!* Edmonton: Edmonton Social Planning Council/ Edmonton Gleaners' Association.

Elliot, D., and N. Johnson. 1983. "Fetal Alcohol Syndrome: Implications and Counselling Considerations." *Personnel and Guidance Journal* (October): 67–69.

Ellison Williams, E., and F. Williams. 1996. "Culturally Informed Social Work Practice with American Indian Clients: Guidelines for Non-Indian Social Workers. *Social Work* 41(2): 147–51.

Erickson, F. 1996. "Going for the Zone: The Social and Cognitive Ecology of Teacher-Student Interaction in Classroom Conversations." In D. Hicks (ed.), *Discourse, Learning and Schooling*. Cambridge: University of Cambridge Press.

Erikson, N. 1993. "Aboriginal Nurses Perspective." *Report on the Community Consultation on Fetal Alcohol Effects and Fetal Alcohol Syndrome*. Winnipeg: Manitoba Medical Association and the Alcoholism Foundation of Manitoba.

Faber, A., and E. Mazlish. 1980. *How To Talk So Kids Will Listen and Listen So Kids Will Talk*. New York: Avon Books.

Fagan, J.F. 1984. "The Relationship of Novelty Preferences During Infancy to Later Intelligence and Later Recognition Memory." *Intelligence* 8: 339–46.

Falconer, Nancy, and K. Swift. 1983. *Preparing for Practice: The Fundamentals*

References

of Child Protection. Toronto: Children's Aid Society of Metropolitan Toronto.

Ferber, R. 1985. *Solve Your Child's Sleep Problems.* New York: Simon and Schuster.

Finlay, G., and A. Sorenson. 1995. "What Educators Need to Know About Having Students with Fetal Alcohol Syndrome and Fetal Alcohol Effects in the Classroom: Issues, Identification, Intervention and Instructional Strategies." ERIC Document Reproduction Service no. ED 385 039. Charlottesville, Va: Curry School of Education, University of Virginia.

Frankenburg, W.K., J. Dodds, P. Archer, H. Shapiro and B. Bresnick. 1992. "The Denver II: A Major Revision and Restandardization of the Denver Developmental Screening Test." *Pediatrics* 89: 91.

Garber, S., M. Daniels Garber and R. Freedman Spitzman. 1997. *Beyond Ritalin.* New York: Harper Collins.

Garret, M.T., and J.E. Myers. 1996. "The Rule of Opposites: A Paradigm for Counselling Native Americans." *Journal of Multicultural Counseling and Development* 24(2): 89–104.

Garshelis, J., and S. McConnel. 1993. "Comparison of Family Needs Assessed by Mothers, Individual Professionals, and Interdisciplinary Teams. *Journal of Early Intervention* 17(1): 36–49.

Given, B., C. Given and A. Harlan. 1994. "Strategies to Meet the Needs of the Rural Poor." *Seminars in Oncology Nursing* 10(2): 114–22.

Gove, T. 1995. *Matthew's Legacy: Report of the Gove Inquiry into Child Protection.* British Columbia: Ministry of Social Services.

Grant, T., C. Ernst, A. Streissguth, P. Phillips and B. Gendler. 1996. "When Case Management Isn't Enough: A Model of Paraprofessional Advocacy for Drug and Alcohol Abusing Mothers." *Journal of Case Management* 5(1): 3–11.

Guinta, C., and A. Streissguth. 1988. "Patients with Fetal Alcohol Syndrome and Their Caretakers." *Social Casework: The Journal of Contemporary Social Work*: 453–59.

Halfon, N., G. Berkowitz and L. Klee. 1993. "Development of an Integrated Case Management Program for Vulnerable Children." *Child Welfare* 72(4): 379–96.

Hampton, M., E. Hampton, G. Kinunwa and L. Kinunwa. 1995. "Alaska Recovery and Spirit Camps: First Nations Community Development." *Community Development Journal* 30(3): 257–64.

Harper, D.C., and D.P. Wacker. 1983. "The Efficiency of the Denver Developmental Screening Test with Rural Disadvantaged Preschool Children." *Journal of Pediatric Psychology* 8: 273–83.

Hennessy, J.J., and P.R. Merrifield. 1976. "A Comparison of the Factor Structures of Mental Abilities in Four Ethnic Groups." *Journal of Educational Psychology* 68: 754–59.

Herrnstein, R.J., and C. Murray. 1994. *The Bell Curve: Intelligence and Class Structure in American Life.* New York: Free Press.

Hicks, D. 1995. "Discourse, Learning, and Teaching." *Review of Research in Education* 21: 49–98.

Huxley, P. 1993. "Case Management and Care Management in Community Care." *British Journal of Social Work* 23(4): 365–81.

Ingersoll, B. 1988. *Your Hyperactive Child*. Toronto: Doubleday.

Institute of Medicine. 1996. *Fetal Alcohol Syndrome: Diagnosis, Epidemiology, Prevention and Treatment*. Washington, D.C.: Institute of Medicine.

Iwawaki, S., and P. Vernon. 1988. "Japanese Abilities and Achievements." In S.H. Irvine and J.W. Berry (eds.), *Human Abilities in Cultural Context*. New York: Cambridge University Press.

Jacobson, J., S. Jacobson, R. Sokol, S. Martier, J. Ager and M. Kaplan-Estrin. 1993. "Teratogenic Effects of Alcohol on Infant Development." *Alcoholism: Clinical and Experimental Research* 17: 174–83.

Janzen, H.L., S. Skakum and W. Lightning. 1994. "Professional Services in a Cree Native Community." *Canadian Journal of School Psychology* 10(1): 88–102.

Janzen, L., J. Nanson and G. Block. 1995. "Neuropsychological Evaluation of Preschoolers with Fetal Alcohol Syndrome." *Neurotoxicology and Teratology* 17: 273–79.

Jensen, A., and F. McGurk. 1987. "Black-White Bias in 'Cultural' and 'Noncultural' Test Items." *Personality and Individual Differences* 8: 295–301.

Jones, K. 1997. *Smith's Recognizable Patterns of Human Malformation*. Fifth edition. Toronto: Sanders and Co.

—————, D. Smith, C. Ulleland and A. Streissguth. 1973. "Pattern of Malformation in Offspring of Chronic Alcoholic Mothers." *Lancet* 1: 1267–71.

Jones, R., C. McCullough and M. Dewoody. 1992. "The Child Welfare Challenges in Meeting Developmental Needs." *Identifying the Needs of Drug-Affected Children: Public Policy Issues*. OSAP monograph no. 11. Maryland: U.S. Department of Health and Human Services.

Kagan, J., D. Arcus and N. Snidman. 1993. "The Idea of Temperament: Where Do We Go from Here?" In R. Plomin and G.E. McClearn (eds.), *Nature, Nurture & Psychology*. Washington, D.C.: American Psychological Association.

Karp, R., Q. Qutub, K. Moller, W. Angelo and J. Davis. 1995. "Fetal Alcohol Syndrome at the Turn of the 20th Century." *Archives of Pediatric Medicine* 149: 45–48.

King, W. 1991. "Study Cites Alcohol Damage to Unborn." *Seattle Times*, April 16, B1.

Kleinfeld, J., and S. Wescott, eds. 1993. *Fantastic Antone Succeeds!* Alaska: University of Alaska Press.

Kodituwakku, P., N. Handmaker, S. Cutler, E. Weathersby and S. Handmaker. 1995. "Specific Impairments in Self-Regulation in Children Exposed to Alcohol Prenatally." *Alcoholism: Clinical and Experimental Research* 19: 1558–64.

Kovalesky, A., 1997. "Child Placement Issues of Women with Addictions." *Journal of Obstetric, Gynecologic and Neonatal Nursing* 26(5): 585–91.

LaFromboise, T.D. 1988. "American Indian Mental Health Policy." *American Psychologist* 43: 388–97.

Lemoine, P., H. Harousseau, J. Borteyru and J. Menuet. 1968. "Children of Alcoholic Parents: Abnormalities Observed in 127 Cases." *Quest Medical* 21: 476–92.

Lezak, M. 1995. *Neuropsychological Assessment*. Third edition. New York: Oxford

References

University Press.

Lindsay, A. 1997. "Exploring Dyadic Classroom Discourse: Tracking and Mapping the Talk." Paper presented at the Canadian Society for the Study of Education Conference, Memorial University, St. John's, N.F., June 1997.

Little, B., L. Snell, C. Rosenfeld, L. Gilstrap and N. Grant. 1990. "Failure to Recognize Fetal Alcohol Syndrome in Newborn Infants." *American Journal of Diseases of Children* 144: 1142–46.

Lutke, J. 1995. "Fetal Alcohol Syndrome/Effect and Children in the 'System'." Paper presented at workshop of the Cooperative University-Provincial Psychiatric Liaison, University of British Columbia, Vancouver, B.C., November 1995.

——————. 1993. "Parental advocacy for alcohol-affected children." In J. Kleinfeld and S. Wescott (eds.), *Fantastic Antone Succeeds!* Alaska: University of Alaska Press.

Lynn, R. 1991. "Race Differences in Intelligence: A Global Perspective." *Mankind Quarterly* 31: 254–96.

Majewski, F., and T. Goecke. 1982. "Alcohol Embryopathology." In E. Abel (ed.), *Fetal Alcohol Syndrome. Vol. 11: Human Studies*. Florida: CRC Press.

Mann, E., Y. Ikeda, C. Mueller, A. Takahashi, K. Tao, E. Humris, B. Li and D. Chin. 1992. "Cross-Cultural Differences in Rating Hyperactive-Disruptive Behaviors in Children." *American Journal of Psychiatry* 149: 1539–42.

Matarazzo, J.D. 1972. *Wechsler's Measurement and Appraisal of Adult Intelligence*. New York: Oxford University Press.

Mattson, S., E. Riley, D. Delis, C. Stern and K. Jones. 1996. "Verbal Learning and Memory in Children with Fetal Alcohol Syndrome." *Alcoholism: Clinical and Experimental Research* 20: 810–16.

Mawhiney, A.M. 1995. "The First Nations in Canada." In J.C. Turner and F.J. Turner (eds.), *Canadian Social Welfare*. Third edition. Scarborough, Ont.: Allyn and Bacon.

May, P.A. 1988. "The Health Status of Indian Children: Problems and Prevention in Early Life." In S.M. Manson and N.G. Dinges (eds.), *Behavioral Health Issues Among American Indians and Alaska Natives*. Monograph no. 1. Denver, Colo.: National Center for American Indian and Alaska Native Mental Health Research.

McCall, R.B.. 1979. "The Development of Intellectual Functioning in Infancy and the Prediction of Later IQ." In J.D. Osofsky (ed.), *Handbook of Infant Development*. New York: Wiley.

——————. 1977. "Childhood IQs as Predictors of Adult Educational and Occupational Status." *Science* 197: 482–83.

McCormick, R. 1995. "The Facilitating of Healing for the First Nations People of British Columbia." *Canadian Journal of Native Education* 21(2): 251–322.

McShane, D., and J.W. Berry. 1988. "Native North Americans: Indian and Inuit abilities." In S.H. Irvine and J.W. Berry (eds.), *Human Abilities in Cultural Context*. New York: Cambridge University Press.

Morgan, S. 1985. *Children in Crisis: A Team Approach to Schools*. San Diego: College-Hill Press.

Morrissette, V., B. McKenzie and L. Morrissette. 1993. "Towards an Aboriginal Model of Social Work Practice: Cultural Knowledge and Traditional Practices."

Canadian Social Work Review 10(1): 91–108.

Nanson, J.L., and M. Hiscock. 1990. "Attention Deficits in Children Exposed to Alcohol Prenatally." *Alcoholism: Clinical and Experimental Research* 14: 656–61.

National Anti-Poverty Organization (NAPO). 1997. "Monitoring the Impacts on Social Assistance Recipients of Welfare Cuts and Changes: An Update, March 21, 1997." Ottawa: NAPO.

National Center for Education Statistics. 1991. *Trends in Academic Progress: Achievement of American Students in Science 1970–90, Mathematics 1973–90, Reading 1971–90, and Writing 1984–90.* Washington, D.C.: National Center for Education Statistics.

National Council of Welfare (NCW). 1997. *Another Look at Welfare Reform.* Ottawa: Minister of Public Works and Government Services Canada.

——————. 1996. *Poverty Profile 1994.* Ottawa: Minister of Supply and Services.

——————. 1995. *Poverty Profile 1993.* Ottawa: Minister of Supply and Services.

Nelson, C.H., M.L. Kelley and D.H. McPherson. 1985. "Rediscovering Support in Social Work Practice: Lessons from Indigenous Human Service Workers." *Canadian Social Work Review* 1: 231–48.

Osborne, J. 1994. *A Sourcebook of Successful School-Based Strategies for Fetal Alcohol and Drug-Affected Students.* ERIC Document Reproduction Service no. ED 380 719. Portland, Ore.: Western Regional Center for Drug-Free Schools and Communities.

Pappas, C., B. Kiefer and L. Levstik. 1995. *An Integrated Language Perspective in the Elementary School.* Second edition. White Plains, N.Y.: Longman.

Peat, F.D. 1994. *Lighting the Seventh Fire: The Spiritual Ways, Healing, and Science of the Native American.* Toronto: Canadian Manda Group.

Phelan, T. 1995. *1-2-3 Magic.* Second edition. Illinois: Quality Books.

Polanka, W. 1969. "Using Ward Personnel as Case Managers." *Hospital and Community Psychiatry* 20: 93–95.

Pulkingham, J. 1997 (forthcoming). "Remaking the Social Divisions of Welfare: Gender, 'Dependency,' and UI Reform." *Studies in Political Economy*, no. 56.

—————— and G. Ternowetsky. 1997. "The Changing Context of Child and Family Policies." In J. Pulkingham and G. Ternowetsky (eds.), *Child and Family Policies: Struggles, Strategies and Options.* Halifax: Fernwood.

—————— and G. Ternowetsky. 1996. "The Changing Landscape of Social Policy and the Canadian Welfare State." In J. Pulkingham and G. Ternowetsky (eds.), *Remaking Canadian Social Policy: Social Security in the Late 1990s.* Halifax: Fernwood.

Quinn, R., and J. Stern. 1991. *Putting On the Brakes.* New York: Magination Press.

Rapp, C., and R. Chamberlain. 1985. "Case Management Services for the Chronic Mentally Ill." *Social Work* 30: 417–22.

Regnier, R. 1995. "The Sacred Circle: A Process Pedagogy of Healing." *Interchange* 25(2): 129–44.

Robinson, G., J. Conry and R. Conry. 1987. "Clinical Profile and Prevalence of Fetal Alcohol Syndrome in an Isolated Community in British Columbia."

References

Canadian Medical Association Journal 137(August): 203–7.

Rothman, J. 1991. "A Model of Case Management: Towards Empirically Based Practice." *National Association of Social Workers* 36(6): 520–28.

Sattler, J.M. 1988. *Assessment of Children.* Third edition. San Diego: Jerome Sattler.

Schilling, R., S. Schinke and R. Weatherly. 1988. "Service Trends in a Conservative Era: Social Workers Rediscover the Past." *Social Work* (January-February): 5–9.

Schmidt, F.L., and D.S. Ones. 1992. "Personnel selection." *Annual Review of Psychology* 43: 627–70.

Schmidt, G., and J. Turpin. 1996. "Towards a Case Management Model with FAS/E Children in Northern and Remote Communities." In G. Schmidt and J. Turpin (eds.), *Fetal Alcohol Syndrome/Fetal Alcohol Effects: A Resource Manual.* Prince George, B.C.: Child Welfare Research Centre, University of Northern British Columbia.

Shore, J.H., and S.M. Manson. 1981. "Cross-Cultural Studies of Depression Among American Indians and Alaska Natives." *White Cloud Journal* 2: 5–12.

Smith, I. 1992. "An Ecological Perspective: The Impact of Culture and Social Environment on Drug Exposed Children." In *Identifying the Needs of Drug-Affected Children: Public Policy Issues.* OSAP monograph no. 11. Maryland: U.S. Department of Health and Human Services.

Smitherman, C. 1994. "The Lasting Impact of Fetal Alcohol Syndrome and Fetal Alcohol Effects on Children and Adolescents." *Journal of Pediatric Health Care* 8(1): 121–26.

Social Planning Council of Metropolitan Toronto (SPCMT). 1996. "Ontario's Welfare Rate Cuts: An Anniversary Report." Toronto: SPCMT. (http://www.worldchat.com/public/tab/owrc1/htm).

Sparks, S. 1993. *Children of Prenatal Substance Abuse: School Age Children Series.* California: Singular.

Statistics Canada. 1997. "Regular Beneficiaries Without Earnings and Unemployed." *Unemployment Insurance Monthly Statistics.* Ottawa: Statistics Canada Labour Division.

Streissguth, A., 1996. *Understanding the Occurrence of Secondary Disabilities in Clients with Fetal Alchol Syndrome (FAS) and Fetal Alcohol Effects (FAE): Final Report.* Available from the Fetal Alcohol and Drug Unit, Seattle, Washington.

—————. 1994. "Reflections on Fetal Alcohol Syndrome: A Conversation with Dr. Paul Lemoine, M.D., Nantes, France." *Iceberg* 4(1): 4–5.

—————, J. Aase, S. Clarren, S. Randels, R. Ladue and D. Smith. 1991. "Fetal Alcohol Syndrome in Adolescents and Adults." *Journal of the American Medical Association* 265(15): 1961–67.

—————, H. Barr, H. Olson, P. Sampson, F. Bookstein and D. Burgess. 1994. "Drinking During Pregnancy Decreases Word Attack and Arithmetic Scores on Standardized Tests: Adolescent Data from a Population-Based Prospective Study." *Alcoholism: Clinical and Experimental Research* 18: 248–54.

—————, S. Clarren and K. Jones. 1985. "Natural History of the Fetal

Alcohol Syndrome: A 10-Year Follow-Up Study of 11 Patients." *Lancet* (2): 85–92.

—————— and C. Guinta. 1988. "Symposium on Addiction and the Family: Mental Health and Health Needs of Infants and Preschool Children with FAS." *International Journal of Family Psychiatry* 9(1): 29–47.

Struthers, J. 1996. *Can Workfare Work? Reflections from History.* Ottawa: Caledon Institute of Social Policy. (http://www.cyberplus.ca/~caledon/welfare.htm).

Sue, D.W., A.E. Ivey and P.B. Pedersen. 1996. *A Theory of Multicultural Counseling and Therapy.* Toronto: Brooks/Cole.

Sue, S., and S. Okazaki. 1990. "Asian-American Educational Achievemencs: A Phenomenon in Search of an Explanation." *American Psychologist* 45: 913–20.

Teichroeb, R. 1997. "Women's Voices Expose FAS Epidemic: Natives Breaking Taboo About Fetal Alcohol Syndrome." *Winnipeg Free Press*, February 26, A5.

Timpson, J., S. McKay, S. Kakegamic, D. Roundhead, C. Cohen and G. Matewapit. 1988. "Depression in a Native Canadian in Northwestern Ontario: Sadness, Grief or Spiritual Illness?" *Canada's Mental Health* (June/September): 5–8.

Tobias, J.L. 1991. "Protection, Civilization, Assimilation: An Outline History of Canada's Indian Policy." In J.R. Miller (ed.), *Sweet Promises: A Reader on Indian-White Relations in Canada.* Toronto: University of Toronto Press.

Torjman, S. 1995. *The Let-Them-Eat-Cake Law.* Ottawa: Caledon Institute of Social Policy.

—————— and K. Battle. 1995. *The Dangers of Block Funding.* Ottawa: Caledon Institute of Social Policy.

Turpin, J. 1996. *Fetal Alcohol Syndrome/Fetal Alcohol Effects: What Do Child Protection Workers Know?* Unpublished M.S.W. thesis, University of Northern British Columbia.

Uecker, A., and L. Nadel. 1996. "Spatial Locations Gone Awry: Object and Spatial Memory Deficits in Children with Fetal Alcohol Syndrome." *Neuropsychologia* 34: 209–23.

Valencia, R.R., and R.J. Rankin. 1988. "Evidence of Bias in Predictive Validity on the Kaufman Assessment Battery for Children in Samples of Anglo and Mexican American Children." *Psychology in the Schools* 25: 257–66.

Valpy, M. 1997. "A Down Payment, But Where Does It Lead?" *The Globe and Mail,* February 20, A21.

Van Bibber, M. 1992. "Report from the Aboriginal Participants." *Report on the Symposium on Fetal Alcohol Syndrome and Fetal Alcohol Effects*, Vancouver, September 30 to October . Ottawa: Minister of Health and Welfare.

VanderVeer, B., and E. Schweid. 1974. "Infant Assessment: Stability of Mental Functioning in Young Retarded Children." *American Journal of Mental Deficiency* 79: 1–4.

Vernon, P, D. Jackson and S. Messick. 1988. "Cultural Influences on Patterns of Abilities in North America." In S.H. Irvine and J.W. Berry (eds.), *Human Abilities in Cultural Context.* New York: Cambridge University Press.

Vourlekis, Betsy, and R. Greene, eds. 1992. *Social Work Case Management.* New York: Aldine de Gruyter.

Weick, A. 1983. "Issues in Overturning a Medical Model of Social Work Practice."

References

Social Work 28(6): 467–71.

Weisz, J., S. Suwanlert, W. Chaiyasit and B. Walter. 1987. "Over and Undercontrolled Referral Problems Among Children and Adolescents from Thailand and the United States: The Wat and Wai of Cultural Differences." *Journal of Consulting and Clinical Psychology* 55: 719–26.

Wells, G., and G. Chang-Wells. 1992. *Constructing Knowledge Together.* Portsmouth, N.H.: Heinemann.

Willard, C. 1970. "Psychiatric Aides as Case Managers." *Hospital and Community Psychiatry* 21: 93.

World Health Organization (WHO). 1992. *The ICD-10 Classification of Mental and Behavioral Disorders: Clinical Descriptions and Diagnostic Guidelines.* Geneva, Switzerland: WHO.

—————. 1983. *Depressive Disorders in Different Cultures.* Geneva, Switzerland: WHO.

—————. 1973. *International Pilot Study of Schizophrenia.* Geneva, Switzerland: WHO.

Zaleski, W.A. 1983. "Fetal Alcohol Effects: The Saskatchewan Experience." *Proceedings of a National Symposium on Fetal Alcohol Syndrome.* Winnipeg: University of Manitoba.

Zapf, M.K. 1985. *Rural Social Work and Its Application to the Canadian North as a Practice Setting.* Toronto: University of Toronto Faculty of Social Work.